Chartered Institute for Securities

Level 3

Investment Operations Certificate (IOC™)

Introduction to Securities and Investment

Practice and Revision Kit

July 2013

Syllabus version 13

Contents

	Page
Question Bank	1
Practice Examinations	77

A note about copyright

Dear Customer

What does the little © mean and why does it matter?
Your market-leading BPP books, course materials and e-learning materials do not write and update themselves. People write them: on their own behalf or as employees of an organisation that invests in this activity. Copyright law protects their livelihoods. It does so by creating rights over the use of the content. Breach of copyright is a form of theft – as well being a criminal offence in some jurisdictions, it is potentially a serious breach of professional ethics.

With current technology, things might seem a bit hazy but, basically, without the express permission of BPP Learning Media:

- Photocopying our materials is a breach of copyright
- Scanning, ripcasting or conversion of our digital materials into different file formats, uploading them to facebook or emailing them to your friends is a breach of copyright

You can, of course, sell your books, in the form in which you have brought them – once you have finished with them. (Is this fair to your fellow students? We update for a reason.) But the e-products are sold on a single user license basis: we do not supply 'unlock' codes to people who have bought them second-hand.

And what about outside the UK? BPP Learning Media strives to make our materials available at prices students can afford by local printing arrangements, pricing policies and partnerships which are clearly listed on our website. A tiny minority ignore this and indulge in criminal activity by illegally photocopying out material or supporting organisations that do. If they act illegally and unethically in on area, can you really trust them?

ISBN: 9781 4453 6576 3
eISBN: 9781 4727 0169 5

Printed in the United Kingdom by Ricoh
Ricoh House, 15 Ullswater Crescent,
Coulsdon, CR5 2HR

© BPP Learning Media – July 2013

No part of this publication may be reproduced, stored in a retrieval system or transmitted, in any form or by any means electronic, mechanical, photocopying, recording or otherwise without the prior permission of BPP Learning Media Ltd. The descriptions, examples and calculations shown in this publication are for educational purposes only. No liability can be accepted by BPP Learning Media Ltd for their use in any circumstances connected with actual trading activity or otherwise. Readers should seek specific advice for specific situations.

Question Bank

Contents

Question Bank		Page number	
		Questions	Answers
Chapter 1	Financial Services and the Economic Environment	3	7
Chapter 2	Equities, Bonds and Money Markets	9	19
Chapter 3	Derivatives	25	29
Chapter 4	Financial Product Types	31	39
Chapter 5	Pooled Investment Funds	45	51
Chapter 6	Financial Services Regulation and Ethics	53	61
Chapter 7	Tax, ISAs and Trusts	65	73

1. Financial Services and the Economic Environment

Questions

1. **Which of the following measures the total value of goods and services produced within the UK?**

    A   PSNCR
    B   GDP
    C   CPI
    D   GDP deflator

2. **Which one of these services would a third party administrator not provide?**

    A   Consolidated reporting
    B   Trade execution
    C   Custody
    D   International settlement

3. **Which of the following statements is the most relevant to a market economy?**

    A   Facilitating international trade helps people's needs to be met
    B   Markets are driven by levels of supply and demand
    C   Economic growth is enhanced through central planning
    D   The price mechanism is central to the allocation of resources

4. **Which one of the following statements is true of the public sector net cash requirement?**

    A   It represents the net deficit on the UK's balance of payments
    B   It represents the total taxes collected by the government
    C   It is funded through the issue of gilts
    D   It is a measure of inflation

5. **Which of the following would not be included in GDP figures in the UK?**

    I   Earnings from tourism
    II   Income generated by financial sector
    III   Work carried out on a property by its owner
    IV   Work carried out for cash in hand by a person who does not declare the income

    A   I, III and IV only
    B   I and II only
    C   III and IV only
    D   II and III only

6. **Which of the following statements is true?**

   A The Monetary Policy Committee sets the UK inflation target
   B Falling retail sales would indicate inflationary pressure in the economy
   C Tourism is not an aspect of the balance of payments
   D The RPI includes mortgage payments

7. **Which one of the following best describes the function of a custodian?**

   A A firm that deals and settles on an investor's behalf and then holds the security in title
   B A firm that offers settlement and corporate action processing services to investors
   C A firm that simply credits security income to an investor's account on the contracted date
   D A firm that invests clients' money on a discretionary basis

8. **Which of the following own or owns the London Stock Exchange?**

   A The Bank of England
   B The Financial Conduct Authority
   C The LSE's shareholders
   D HM Treasury

9. **Which one of the following is true of ICE Futures Europe?**

   A It is a trading platform for soft commodity derivatives
   B It is a trading platform for financial derivatives
   C It is a trading platform for energy derivatives
   D It is regulated by the Securities and Exchange Commission

10. **On which of the following exchanges can you trade US equities in euros?**

    A Deutsche Börse
    B EUREX
    C LIFFE
    D Deutsche Terminbörse

11. **In the UK, how would you expect the current account typically to appear in the balance of payments?**

    A Visibles in deficit, invisibles in surplus
    B Visibles in deficit, invisibles in deficit
    C Visibles in surplus, invisibles in deficit
    D Visibles in surplus, invisibles in surplus

12. Which of the following is not a function of the Bank of England?

    A Setting of interest rates via the MPC
    B Maintaining stability in the financial system
    C Responsible for conduct regulation in the financial services industry
    D Oversight of settlement and payment systems

13. Which of the following exchanges is not part of NYSE Euronext?

    A Amsterdam
    B Berlin
    C Paris
    D Brussels

14. Which one of the following would reduce the Public Sector Net Cash Requirement?

    A Increasing corporate taxation
    B Printing money
    C Borrowing from abroad
    D Selling Treasury bills to UK residents

15. Which of the following represents a measure of inflation in the UK that is harmonised with European inflationary measures?

    A CPI
    B RPIX
    C RPIY
    D HIRP

16. Which of the following is true of NASDAQ?

    A It is an order-driven market
    B It is a market primarily for trading American derivatives
    C It is a market primarily for technology and innovative companies
    D Only fully listed companies may trade on NASDAQ

17. The category of retail investment products most closely defines the range of products on which advice will be provided by

    A An adviser offering independent advice
    B An adviser offering restricted advice
    C An adviser offering basic advice using pre-scripted questions
    D A product provider

18. **Spot currency transactions are normally settled within**
    A One business day (T + 1)
    B Two business days (T + 2)
    C Three business days (T + 3)
    D Five business days (T + 5)

19. **Settlement for foreign currency forward deals is generally**
    A One business day (T + 1)
    B Two business days (T + 2)
    C Three business days (T + 3)
    D The day agreed by the participants to the transaction

20. **The foreign exchange markets in the UK are dominated by**
    A Banks
    B Lloyd's of London
    C Money brokers
    D Independent brokers

21. **UK equities can be traded on**
    A LSE
    B NYSE LIFFE
    C ICE Futures
    D LME

22. **What is the name of the trade body for the UK fund management industry?**
    A Association of Investment Funds
    B Asset Management Institute
    C Association of UK Asset Managers
    D Investment Management Association

23. **The Financial Policy Committee**
    A Decides on the level of benchmark interest rates
    B Is the conduct regulator for dual-regulated firms
    C Is responsible for macro-prudential regulation
    D Is an EU body which co-ordinates with national regulators

1 ♦ Financial Services and the Economic Environment – Answers

Answers

1. **B** GDP or Gross Domestic Product. GNP or Gross National Product refers to goods and services produced by the nationals of a particular country

   BPP Study Text Chapter 1 Section 1.9.1 / CISI Workbook Chapter 1 Section 5.2.1

2. **B** Third party administrators (TPAs) provide back office services, ie after the trade is done. Hence they would not execute trades for their clients

   BPP Study Text Chapter 1 Section 3.11 / CISI Workbook Chapter 1 Section 4.11

3. **B** Central planning of production is a feature of a State-controlled economy, while a market economy involves much less State intervention. In a market economy resource allocation determined is by the price mechanism, through the dynamic forces of supply and demand. Trade is one aspect of the free market, which generally enables people's needs to be met

   BPP Study Text Chapter 1 Section 1.3 / CISI Workbook Chapter 2 Section 2.2

4. **C** The balance of payments is the difference between imports and exports. PSNCR is the difference between government spending and tax revenues

   BPP Study Text Chapter 1 Section 1.9.3 / CISI Workbook Chapter 2 Section 5.2.4

5. **C** III and IV will not be recorded and thus will not form part of the Gross Domestic Product calculation

   BPP Study Text Chapter 1 Section 1.9.1 / CISI Workbook Chapter 1 Section 5.2.1

6. **D** The MPC sets interest rates, not inflation. The inflation target is set by the Chancellor

   BPP Study Text Chapter 1 Sections 1.8.1 and 2.2.4 / CISI Workbook Chapter 2 Section 3.2.1

7. **B** Custodians generally offer safekeeping, settlement and corporate action processing services to their clients but do not normally deal for their clients. In other words, they do more than just credit a client's account with income on a contracted date. Custodians do not normally take investment decisions

   BPP Study Text Chapter 1 Section 3.9 / CISI Workbook Chapter 1 Sections 2 and 4.9

8. **C** Since its demutualisation, the LSE has been a plc and so, like any other plc, it is owned by its shareholders

   BPP Study Text Chapter 1 Section 4.1 / CISI Workbook Chapter 4 Section 8.2.1

9. **C** ICE Futures is owned by IntercontinentalExchange (ICE) and is for the trading of energy derivatives. Soft commodities comprise agricultural products and foodstuffs

   BPP Study Text Chapter 1 Section 5.2 / CISI Workbook Chapter 6 Section 5.2.1

10. **A** Deutsche Börse deals with equities. (Deutsche Terminbörse is the former name of Eurex.)

    BPP Study Text Chapter 1 Section 6.5 / CISI Workbook Chapter 4 Section 8.2.3

11. **A** Visible trade is trade conducted in physical goods; invisibles are trades in services and income flows

    BPP Study Text Chapter 1 Section 1.9.2 / CISI Workbook Chapter 2 Section 5.2.3

1 ♦ Financial Services and the Economic Environment – Answers

12.	C	It is the FCA that is responsible for conduct regulation in the industry

BPP Study Text Chapter 1 Section 2.2 / CISI Workbook Chapter 2 Section 3.2

13.	B	NYSE Euronext is the second largest exchange in Europe, behind the LSE

BPP Study Text Chapter 1 Sections 5.1 and 6.2 / CISI Workbook Chapter 4 Section 8.2.2

14.   A   Government spending over and above the money collected from taxation represents the PSNCR. Thus, if more money is collected by taxing businesses, the PSNCR will reduce

BPP Study Text Chapter 1 Section 1.9.3 / CISI Workbook Chapter 2 Section 5.2.4

15.   A   The Consumer Prices Index is a measure of consumer price inflation, calculated using methodology similar to that used in the rest of Europe

BPP Study Text Chapter 1 Section 1.8.2 / CISI Workbook Chapter 2 Section 5.1

16.   C   As one of the largest electronic quote-driven markets in the world, NASDAQ specialises in offering a trading platform for technology and innovative companies

BPP Study Text Chapter 1 Section 6.3 / CISI Workbook Chapter 4 Section 8.1.2

17.   A   An independent adviser will need to provide unbiased, unrestricted advice based on a comprehensive and fair analysis of the relevant market. To reflect the range of products that a consumer would expect an independent adviser to have knowledge of, the regulator has introduced the term 'retail investment product'

BPP Study Text Chapter 1 Section 9.1 / CISI Workbook Chapter 1 Section 5.1

18.   B   Note that these are business days not calendar days

BPP Study Text Chapter 1 Section 7.2 / CISI Workbook Chapter 3 Section 5

19.   D   Each forward is tailored to suit the counterparties' needs, hence there is no fixed settlement date – parties agree a date unique to that forward transaction

BPP Study Text Chapter 1 Section 7.3 / CISI Workbook Chapter 3 Section 5

20.   A   The large and informal forex markets are dominated by the major banks

BPP Study Text Chapter 1 Section 7.1 / CISI Workbook Chapter 3 Section 5

21.   A   LIFFE is for the trading of futures and options of shares; ICE Futures is for the trading of energy derivative products; the LME is for trading metal derivatives

BPP Study Text Chapter 1 Sections 4.1 and 4.3 / CISI Workbook Chapter 1 Section 3.1

22.   D   The IMA is the trade body for the UK asset management industry

BPP Study Text Chapter 1 Section 3.11 / CISI Workbook Chapter 1 Section 4.10

23.   C   The FPC is a committee of the Bank of England with responsibility for regulation of the stability and resilience of the financial system as a whole. The Monetary Policy Committee (MPC) makes interest rate decisions (Option A). The FCA is the conduct regulator for dual-regulated firms (Option B)

BPP Study Text Chapter 1 Section 2.2.3 / CISI Workbook Chapter 8 Section 1.2.1

2. Equities, Bonds and Money Markets

Questions

1. What is the best description of the role of a market maker?

    A Deals as an agent for a customer
    B Buys and sells for the firm during the Mandatory Quote Period
    C Arranges mergers and acquisitions
    D Arranges new issues

2. Which of the following is true of CREST?

    A It provides for confirmation of trades
    B It provides for delivery versus payment
    C It is owned and operated by the Bank of England
    D It only offers facilities for both dematerialised and paper settlement

3. What is the next coupon payment for an investor holding Treasury 8% 2015? It is trading at £118.

    A £4.00
    B £3.70
    C £7.40
    D £8.00

4. Which of the following is another name for UK government bonds?

    A Gilt-edged securities
    B Loan stock
    C Corporate bonds
    D National Savings & Investments

5. A loan is approaching redemption at par value shortly. Which of the following is the price likely to be?

    A Much higher than par
    B Close to par
    C Much lower than par
    D Any of the above (A, B or C)

6. **'LIBOR' refers to the**

    A London Interbank Offered Rate
    B London Interbank Open Rate
    C London International Bank Offered Rate
    D London Internal Bank Offered Rate

7. **Which of the following provides book entry facilities for equities?**

    A Euroclear UK & Ireland
    B SETS
    C SEAQ
    D MarketMatch

8. **Which one of the following is true of Eurobonds?**

    A They can only be issued in a European currency
    B New issues are through syndicates of banks
    C They are usually in registered form
    D A medium-term bond is called a FRA

9. **Which one of the following is not an advantage of investing in gilts?**

    A The credit rating of the UK Government
    B Potential tax-free gains
    C A regular income stream
    D A rise in value as interest rates rise

10. **What is the normal settlement period for fixed interest stocks?**

    A T + 1
    B T + 3
    C T + 5
    D T + 10

11. **Which measure is used as the base to fix the interest rate for a Floating Rate Note?**

    A RPI
    B LIBOR
    C FTSE Index
    D APR

12. **What is SETS?**

    A A trading system
    B A settlement system for overseas equities
    C An electronic trade confirmation system
    D A news dissemination system

13. **Which of the following is not a function of Euroclear UK & Ireland, which operates CREST?**

    A It creates payment obligations
    B It automatically reconciles members' holdings of stock
    C It arranges settlement of registered securities
    D It notifies the company registrar that settlement has taken place

14. **During which hours will SETS have automatic execution?**

    A 8:00-17:15
    B 8:30-17:30
    C 8:50-16:30
    D 8:00-16:30

15. **On which trading platform are fixed interest securities traded?**

    A SEAQ
    B SETS
    C SETSqx
    D CREST

16. **How many market makers must there be in SEAQ securities?**

    A At least one
    B At least two
    C At least three
    D At least four

17. **Which of the following is not one of the types of participant you would expect to find in the CREST system?**

    A Sponsored member
    B Direct member
    C Nominee
    D Market maker

18. Settlement for Eurobonds is usually

A   The business day following the day of dealing
B   The second business day following the day of dealing
C   The third business day following the day of dealing
D   Seven calendar days

19. The difference between the buying and selling price of a share is known as

A   Bid
B   Spread
C   Touch
D   Offer

20. Settlement in UK equity transactions usually takes place via

A   Euroclear UK & Ireland
B   Clearstream
C   The Bank of New York
D   Euroclear

21. Which is most likely to occur as an example of a Eurobond?

A   A French company issuing a €-denominated bond in France
B   A French company issuing a €-denominated bond in US
C   A French company issuing a $-denominated bond in France
D   A French company issuing a $-denominated bond in US

22. Which of the following is another name for equities?

A   Bonds
B   Gilts
C   Shares
D   Warrants

23. The Hang Seng Index covers the stock market of

A   Shanghai
B   Beijing
C   Hong Kong
D   Singapore

24. Which of the following is not a type of money market instrument?

    A Treasury bill
    B Corporate bond
    C Commercial paper
    D Commercial bill

25. The FTSE 100 Index comprises the 100 largest companies measured by reference to

    A Profit
    B Market capitalisation
    C Turnover
    D Share price

26. Which of the following is true of company Memoranda and Articles of Association?

    A The Memorandum is the same as the company's prospectus
    B A Memorandum is no longer required for private companies
    C The Articles deal with the relationship between the company and its members
    D The Articles for a listed company must follow the Companies Act 2006 model articles

27. In what way is investing in preference shares similar to investing in bonds?

    A Have equal security in event of a winding up
    B Dividends on preference shares are usually fixed
    C Both must give the same return
    D Both have equal voting rights

28. Which of the following issues raise funds for the company?

    I   Rights
    II   Scrip
    III Capitalisation
    IV   Loan stock

    A I and IV only
    B II and III only
    C I and III only
    D I, II and III only

29. Calculate the next coupon payment for Treasury 2¼% 2023 trading at £99.30.

    A £1.125
    B £2.25
    C £5.50
    D £22.34

30. What are the two alternative names for a bonus issue?

    I   Scrip
    II   Capitalisation
    III   Premium
    IV   Rights

A I and II
B III and IV
C II and III
D I and III

31. Which of the following is not usually underwritten?

A Rights issue
B Offer for sale
C Offer for subscription
D Deeply discounted rights issue

32. The yield curve demonstrates the relationship between

A Yields on securities and credit risk
B Bond yields and bond coupons
C Fund yields and fund growth
D Bond yields and bond maturities

33. Which of the following best describes price risk?

A It is the only source of risk when buying shares
B It is the risk of adverse price movements in the share
C It is the risk of a company going into liquidation
D It is the risk of a counterparty failing to pay its obligations

34. What is the flat yield of a 6% corporate bond, redeemable in ten years, trading at a market price of £109.50?

A 8.0%
B 5.4%
C 5.5%
D 6.8%

35. **A client read in the newspaper about a gilt named Exchequer 12% 2013-17 and asked you what this description means. You would reply that**

    A The gilt is redeemable at the option of the Government between dates in 2013 and 2017
    B The gilt is redeemable at the option of the Government at dates in the year 2013 or in the year 2017
    C The gilt is redeemable at the option of the investor between 2013 and 2017
    D The gilt is redeemable at the option of the investor in the year 2013 or in the year 2017

36. **What is the standard settlement period for UK equities?**

    A Same day
    B T + 1
    C T + 3
    D T + 5

37. **How is the following gilt classified by the DMO? Treasury 5% 2014, issued in 1989**

    A Short dated
    B Medium dated
    C Long dated
    D Undated

38. **In a market in which share certificates are held in a depository that is the holder of record, this method of holding title is referred to as**

    A Bearer form
    B Immobilisation
    C Decertification
    D Dematerialisation

39. **The most likely reason to issue gilts is that the Government**

    A Needs to fund a current account deficit
    B Needs to fund the PSNCR
    C Needs to control inflation
    D Wishes to win votes at the forthcoming General Election

40. **Which is always true of FRNs?**

    A They are long dated
    B They are short dated
    C They pay floating rate interest
    D They pay fixed rate interest

41. Which of the following is not a benefit of owning shares?

    A Potential capital gains
    B Right to seize assets in the event of liquidation of the company
    C The right to vote at the company's AGM
    D The right to subscribe for new shares in the company when a rights issue is announced

42. The FTSE 250 Index measures the performance (in terms of capitalisation) of

    A The top 250 companies on the London Stock Exchange
    B The top 250 companies in Europe excluding the UK
    C The 250 companies beneath the top 100 on the London Stock Exchange
    D The top 250 companies in Europe including the UK

43. Which is the index most widely used to gauge the performance of UK shares?

    A FTSE Industrial Index
    B CPI
    C FTSE 100
    D DJIA index

44. Which of the following indices represents the second tier of UK listed plcs by market capitalisation?

    A FTSE Ordinary
    B FTSE 100
    C FTSE 250
    D FTSE 350

45. What is the income yield of a Treasury 5% gilt, redeemable in two years, trading at a market price of £98.50?

    A 5.1%
    B 5.0%
    C 6.2%
    D 6.8%

46. What is the minimum percentage of votes that allows shareholders to pass a special resolution?

    A 100%
    B 75%
    C 25%
    D 50%

2 ♦ Equities, Bonds and Money Markets – Questions

47. **The listed public company Herring Gillam plc must hold its next AGM:**

    A Within 15 months of the previous AGM
    B Before the end of any calendar year in which no AGM has yet been held
    C Within six months of its financial year end
    D By no specified date, as an AGM is not mandatory

48. **What is the term for a bond that can be exchanged for ordinary shares in the issuing company?**

    A Covered bond
    B Asset-backed bond
    C Corporate bond
    D Convertible bond

49. **A Treasury 4½% 2015 bond trades at a market value of £107.95. What is the flat yield?**

    A 4.5%
    B 3.1%
    C 5.4%
    D 4.2%

50. **With respect to the UKLA Listing Rules, which one of the following is not a requirement for admission to the full list of the LSE?**

    A The expected market value of shares issued by the company must be at least £700,000
    B All securities issued must be freely transferable
    C The company must have a track record of at least five years
    D On a continuing basis, the company must produce six-month (interim) and full year (final) results information

51. **Where there is a central counterparty involved in the process of clearing and settlement, the central counterparty performs a role in all of the following ways, except which one?**

    A Reducing counterparty risk
    B Increasing transparency by reducing anonymity
    C Reducing failed trades and errors
    D Netting of trades

52. **Which of the following securities is regarded as a bearer security?**

    A Shares
    B Gilts
    C Corporate bonds
    D Eurobonds

53. What is the flat yield of a Treasury 8% gilt, redeemable in five years, trading at a market price of £117.30?

  A 8.0%
  B 5.8%
  C 4.0%
  D 6.8%

Answers

1. **B** Market makers are there to promote liquidity and efficiency in the market and hence constantly buy and sell stock during the MQP

   BPP Study Text Chapter 2 Sections 6.5 / CISI Workbook Glossary: Market maker

2. **B** The CREST system is owned by Euroclear UK & Ireland, not the Bank of England. It can facilitate both dematerialised and paper settlement but offers a number of other services; including corporate actions processing

   BPP Study Text Chapter 2 Section 7 / CISI Workbook Chapter 4 Section 13

3. **A** The next coupon payment may be calculated using the following formula. (The current market price is irrelevant)

   Nominal value × Coupon rate × 0.5 = £100 × 8% × 0.5 = £4

   All gilts except 2½% Consols pay coupons semi-annually. Hence, the 'next' coupon is half the annual coupon

   BPP Study Text Chapter 2 Section 8.2.4 / CISI Workbook Chapter 5 Section 2

4. **A** National Savings & Investments forms part of Government borrowings, but UK Government bonds are specifically known as gilts

   BPP Study Text Chapter 2 Section 8.1 / CISI Workbook Chapter 5 Section 3

5. **B** As a bond approaches the date on which it will be redeemed at par, the market price will get nearer to par

   BPP Study Text Chapter 2 Section 8.2 / CISI Workbook Chapter 5 Section 2

6. **A** The definition of LIBOR is often examined

   BPP Study Text Chapter 2 Section 10.1 / CISI Workbook Chapter 5 Section 4.2.3

7. **A** Book entry facilities mean dematerialised settlement. Euroclear UK & Ireland (EUI) operates CREST, which will electronically settle many types of securities, including equities

   BPP Study Text Chapter 2 Section 7.1 / CISI Workbook Chapter 4 Section 13.2

8. **B** Eurobonds may be in any currency. Variable interest bonds are known as Floating Rate Notes (FRNs). Any debt instrument of medium maturity is usually called a note

   BPP Study Text Chapter 2 Section 9.2 / CISI Workbook Chapter 5 Section 4.4

9. **D** As interest rates rise, the price of gilts and bonds, in general, will fall

   BPP Study Text Chapter 2 Section 8.5 / CISI Workbook Chapter 5 Section 5.1.3

10. **B** Most trades settle T + 3 except for gilts (T + 1). This question assumes that corporate bonds and eurobonds are the fixed interest stocks being discussed

    BPP Study Text Chapter 2 Sections 8.2 and 9 / CISI Workbook Chapter 5 Section 2

11. **B** The floating rate of interest is given by the London Interbank Offered Rate (LIBOR)

    BPP Study Text Chapter 2 Section 9.1 / CISI Workbook Chapter 5 Section 4.2.3

12. **A** SETS is an electronic trading platform of the London Stock Exchange

    BPP Study Text Chapter 2 Section 6.2.1 / CISI Workbook Chapter 4 Section 10.1

2 ♦ Equities, Bonds and Money Markets – Answers

13. B Reconciliations are not automatic but happen on a regular basis
BPP Study Text Chapter 2 Section 7 / CISI Workbook Chapter 4 Section 13

14. D The period between 08:00 and 16:30 is also known as Normal Market Hours
BPP Study Text Chapter 2 Section 6.2.1 / CISI Workbook Chapter 4 Section 10.1

15. A SEAQ is the London Stock Exchange's service for the fixed interest (bond) market and AIM securities that are not traded on either SETS or SETSqx
BPP Study Text Chapter 2 Section 6 / CISI Workbook Chapter 4 Section 10.3

16. B At least two, to ensure that there is some competition between market makers
BPP Study Text Chapter 2 Section 6.5 / CISI Workbook Chapter 4 Section 10.3

17. D All are types of participant except market makers
BPP Study Text Chapter 2 Section 7.4 / CISI Workbook Chapter 4 Section 13.3

18. C Eurobond settlement falls into the international settlement norm of T + 3
BPP Study Text Chapter 2 Sections 9.1 and 9.2 / CISI Workbook Chapter 5 Section 4.4

19. B The spread enables market makers to make profits: they buy in shares at a low price, generally reselling them into the market at a higher price
BPP Study Text Chapter 2 Section 6.5.3 / CISI Workbook Chapter 4 Section 5.2

20. A The bulk of equity trades will settle through Euroclear UK & Ireland (CREST), although there are other settlement systems, and inter-office settlement
BPP Study Text Chapter 2 Section 7.1 / CISI Workbook Chapter 4 Section 13

21. C Note both B and C meet the criteria for Eurobonds, since the country the bond is issued in and the currency of issue are not aligned. However, C is much more likely to happen
BPP Study Text Chapter 2 Section 9.2 / CISI Workbook Chapter 5 Section 4.4

22. C Ordinary shareholders have equal voting rights and an equal right to participate in a dividend should one be declared
BPP Study Text Chapter 2 Section 2.1 / CISI Workbook Chapter 4 Section 3

23. C The Hang Seng covers the stock market of Hong Kong, a Special Administrative Region of China
BPP Study Text Chapter 2 Section 5 / CISI Workbook Chapter 4 Section 9

24. B A corporate bond would be a long-term investment, whereas money market instruments are usually short-term
BPP Study Text Chapter 2 Section 10 / CISI Workbook Chapter 3 Section 3

25. B FTSE 100 includes the top 100 UK companies by market capitalisation (Share price × Number of shares). The FTSE 100 represents approximately 70% of the UK market by value
BPP Study Text Chapter 2 Sections 5.1 and 5.2 / CISI Workbook Chapter 4 Section 9.1

26.	C	Following the Companies Act 2006, the Memorandum has limited significance, while the Articles govern the internal relationships of the company

BPP Study Text Chapter 2 Sections 1.2 and 1.3 / CISI Workbook Chapter 4 Section 2

27.	B	The dividend on preference shares are usually fixed, as are the coupons on most bonds, unless of course they are floating rate

BPP Study Text Chapter 2 Section 2.2 / CISI Workbook Chapter 4 Section 3.2

28.	A	Rights issues and loan stock issues raise funds for the company

BPP Study Text Chapter 2 Sections 3.2, 3.3 and 9.1 / CISI Workbook Chapter 4 Section 6

29.	A	The next coupon payment can be calculated as follows. The next coupon payment is half the annual coupon payment

Nominal value × Coupon rate × 0.5 = £100 × 2.25% × 0.5

= £1.125

BPP Study Text Chapter 2 Section 8.2.4 / CISI Workbook Chapter 5 Section 2

30.	A	Bonus issues are also known as capitalisation or scrip issues

BPP Study Text Chapter 2 Section 3.2 / CISI Workbook Chapter 4 Section 6

31.	D	Deeply discounted rights issues are not underwritten

BPP Study Text Chapter 2 Section 3.4.3 / CISI Workbook Chapter 4 Section 6

32.	D	The yield curve demonstrates the relationship between bond yields and their maturities

BPP Study Text Chapter 2 Section 9.8 / CISI Workbook Chapter 5 Section 5.2.1

33.	B	Price risk is the primary source of market risk and arises due to adverse changes in the share price. (Bear in mind that a share buyer also faces liquidity and credit/counterparty risk)

BPP Study Text Chapter 2 Section 2.7 / CISI Workbook Chapter 4 Section 5.1

34.	C	The flat yield is calculated by dividing the annual coupon (in cash terms) by the market price of the bond. Therefore:

£6 coupon/£109.50 price × 100 = 5.48% return

ie for an investment of £110, the investor will receive an annual coupon of £6 (gross), which is an effective return of his money of 5.5% (rounded up)

BPP Study Text Chapter 2 Section 9.7 / CISI Workbook Chapter 5 Section 5.2

35.	A	With a dual-dated bond, the Government has the choice over which date to redeem the gilt

BPP Study Text Chapter 2 Section 8.4 / CISI Workbook Chapter 5 Section 3.1.2

36.	C	Equities settle at T + 3

BPP Study Text Chapter 2 Section 7.2 / CISI Workbook Glossary: T+3

37.	A	Maturity is measured from today until maturity (2014) and thus it is short-dated. The issue date is not relevant

BPP Study Text Chapter 2 Section 8.4 / CISI Workbook Chapter 5 Section 3.2

38.	B	Immobilisation is common in markets that previously relied on physical share certificates, but the certificates are now immobilised in a depository, which is the holder of record in the register

BPP Study Text Chapter 2 Section 2.8 / CISI Workbook Chapter 4 Section 11

39.	B	The Government generally requests that the DMO issues gilts to fund the PSNCR, rather than simply print money or raise taxes

BPP Study Text Chapter 2 Section 8.3 / CISI Workbook Chapter 2 Section 5.2.4

40.	C	They may be short- or long-dated but they will pay floating rate interest

BPP Study Text Chapter 2 Section 9.1 / CISI Workbook Chapter 5 Section 4.2.3

41.	B	Ordinary shareholders will participate equally when a company is wound up – but only if any monies remain

BPP Study Text Chapter 2 Sections 2.1 / CISI Workbook Chapter 4 Section 4

42.	C	The FTSE 250 starts at the 101st largest company by market capitalisation and goes down to the 350th

BPP Study Text Chapter 2 Section 5.2 / CISI Workbook Chapter 4 Section 9.1

43.	C	Answer D refers to the Dow Jones Industrial Average, for the US market, while the CPI measures inflation

BPP Study Text Chapter 2 Section 5.2 / CISI Workbook Chapter 4 Section 9.1

44.	C	The FTSE 250 represents 250 companies after the top 100 companies listed in the UK, which make up the FTSE 100

BPP Study Text Chapter 2 Section 5.2 / CISI Workbook Chapter 4 Section 9.1

45.	A	The flat yield (also known as the income yield) is calculated by dividing the annual coupon (in cash terms) by the market price of the bond. Therefore:

£5 coupon/£98.50 price × 100 = 5.1% return

ie for an investment of £98.50, the investor will receive an annual coupon of £5 (gross), which is an effective return on his money of 5.1%

BPP Study Text Chapter 2 Section 9.7 / CISI Workbook Chapter 5 Section 5.2

46.	B	Special resolutions usually affect shareholders' rights: hence 75% of shareholders need to agree

BPP Study Text Chapter 2 Section 1.4 / CISI Workbook Chapter 4 Section 2.3

47.	C	An AGM is no longer mandatory for a private company, but a listed public company must hold an AGM within six months of the financial year end

BPP Study Text Chapter 2 Section 1.4 / CISI Workbook Chapter 4 Section 2.3

48.	D	A convertible bond is one that can be converted into ordinary shares of the issuing company at the option of the bondholder

BPP Study Text Chapter 2 Section 9 / CISI Workbook Chapter 5 Section 4.2.5

49. **D** The flat yield is calculated as follows.

$$\text{Flat Yield} = \frac{\text{Gross coupon}}{\text{Market price}} \times 100$$

$$= \frac{£4.50}{£107.95} \times 100$$

$$= 4.2\% \text{ to 1 d.p.}$$

BPP Study Text Chapter 2 Section 9.7 / CISI Workbook Chapter 5 Section 5.2

50. **C** The company must have a trading record of at least three years for a Premium listing, although no trading record is required for a Standard listing. In addition to the 'full list' listing rules, the company must agree to meet the continuing obligations of the UKLA Listing Rules. These include publishing information about significant transactions, notifying the LSE of dividend distributions, issuing financial statements, and disclosure of price-sensitive information

BPP Study Text Chapter 2 Section 4.3 / CISI Workbook Chapter 4 Section 7.2.1

51. **B** The central counterparty will more typically enhance pre- and post-trade anonymity, which will tend to reduce transparency

BPP Study Text Chapter 2 Sections 6.2.2 and 6.6 / CISI Workbook Chapter 4 Section 12

52. **D** Eurobonds are generally regarded as 'bearer' securities, as there is no such register of legal ownership held by the issuer. Therefore the 'bearer' of the security is the rightful legal owner. Shares, gilts and corporate bonds are regarded as 'registered' securities, as there is a register identifying legal ownership

BPP Study Text Chapter 2 Section 2.8.1 / CISI Workbook Chapter 5 Section 4.4

53. **D** The flat yield (also known as the income yield) is calculated by dividing the annual coupon (in cash terms) by the market price of the bond. Therefore:

£8 coupon/£117.30 price × 100 = 6.8% return

ie for an investment of £117.30, the investor will receive an annual coupon of £8 (gross), which is an effective return of his money of 6.8%

BPP Study Text Chapter 2 Section 9.7 / CISI Workbook Chapter 5 Section 5.2

3. Derivatives

Questions

1. **In which market conditions does the holder of a put option seek to profit?**

   A Static market
   B Falling market
   C Volatile market
   D Rising market

2. **Which of the following best describes the maximum rewards and risks for the writer of a call option?**

   A Unlimited profit and unlimited loss
   B Limited profit and limited loss
   C Unlimited profit and limited loss
   D Limited profit and unlimited loss

3. **An investor looking to secure a minimum sale price for his assets, but still leave potential for further profit would**

   A Buy a call option
   B Buy a put option
   C Buy a future
   D Sell a future

4. **Which of the following is the best definition of a future?**

   A An obligation to buy a given quantity of an asset on a range of future dates at a predetermined price
   B An agreement to buy or sell a standard quantity of a specified asset on a fixed future date at a price agreed today
   C An agreement to buy or sell a standard quantity of a specified asset on a fixed future date at a price agreed in the future
   D The right to buy or sell a standard quantity of a specified asset on a fixed future date at a price agreed today

5. **The writer of a put option**

   A Expects the share price to fall
   B Expects the share price to rise
   C Will have to return the premium if the option is unexercised
   D Pays the premium

3 ♦ Derivatives – Questions

6. Which one of the following statements is false with regard to options?

   A Call options give the holder the right to buy the underlying share at the prevailing market price at a given date

   B A put option could be bought if an investor held the view that market prices were likely to fall

   C Holders of options pay the premium when opening the position

   D Writers of options are generally looking for price stability

7. A contract that gives the buyer the obligation to pay for the underlying equity on a specified future date is known as

   A A call

   B A put

   C A future

   D A swap

8. Which of the following trades carries potentially unlimited risk?

   A Long future

   B Short future

   C Long call

   D Short put

9. How much does the buyer of an option pay to acquire the right under the option?

   A The premium

   B The strike or exercise price

   C The full nominal value of the contract

   D The tick value for the contract

10. What is meant by a 'call'?

   A The obligation to buy a security at a set price

   B The obligation to sell a security at an unknown price

   C The right to buy a security at a set price

   D The right to sell a security at a set price

11. Selling a put option means you have the

   A Right to buy

   B Right to sell

   C Obligation to buy

   D Obligation to sell

12. **If a put option is exercised, what is the maximum loss to the seller?**

    A Unlimited
    B Premium + Exercise price
    C Premium − Exercise price
    D Premium

13. **Which of the following applies in respect of buying a future?**

    A Obligation to pay seller and deliver underlying
    B Obligation to deliver underlying and receive proceeds
    C Obligation to receive underlying only
    D Obligation to receive underlying and pay seller

14. **Which option has unlimited potential losses?**

    A Long put
    B Short put
    C Long call
    D Short call

15. **Able Limited writes a put option. What would best describe the company's position?**

    A Right to buy shares
    B Obliged to buy if option buyer requests
    C Right to sell the share
    D Obliged to sell if option buyer requests

16. **Which of the following has unlimited risk of losses?**

    A Writer of a call option
    B Holder of a call option
    C Writer of a put option
    D Holder of a put option

17. **An exchange-traded derivative that is settled in cash, and has a fixed price and expiry date, is best described as**

    A A future
    B An option
    C An asset-backed security
    D A forward contract

18. **The amount the buyer of traded options pays upon the purchase of the contract is known as**

    A Collateral
    B Premium
    C Open interest
    D Cash

19. **For which of the following would periodic payments normally cease following the occurrence of a specific event that is contingent on external circumstances?**

    A All swaps
    B Credit default swap
    C Interest rate swap
    D Currency swap

20. **Which of the following is the best description of a party having reason to sell protection through credit default swaps (CDSs)?**

    A An investor wishing to take on additional risk relating to credit events in exchange for income
    B A firm wishing to exchange the risk of borrowing in one currency against the risk of borrowing in another currency
    C A company issuing debt securities which wants to protect itself in the event that it is unable to meet the interest payments due on the securities
    D A party wishing to exchange a floating rate interest rate basis for a fixed rate interest basis

Answers

1. **B** — Holders also need volatility, but B is the best answer for the put buyer

   BPP Study Text Chapter 3 Section 3.3.3 / CISI Workbook Chapter 6 Sections 1.1 and 5.3

2. **D** — The profit is limited to the premium. When you are the writer of a call the potential loss is unlimited. Answer B would be the correct answer for the writer of a put

   BPP Study Text Chapter 3 Section 3.3.2 / CISI Workbook Chapter 6 Sections 1.1 and 5.3

3. **B** — With the put option, where the share price falls, the investor would exercise the put option, and sell the assets, at the exercise price. However, if the underlying share price rises, the investor would simply not exercise his option and keep the asset. If the share price were to rise, and the investor had sold a future, losses would result

   BPP Study Text Chapter 3 Section 3.3.3 / CISI Workbook Chapter 6 Sections 1.1 and 5.3

4. **B** — Answer D is a description of options

   BPP Study Text Chapter 3 Section 2.1 / CISI Workbook Chapter 6 Section 2.2

5. **B** — A writer always receives a premium. The writer of a put will be expecting the price to rise so that the put option will not be exercised against them

   BPP Study Text Chapter 3 Section 3.3.4 / CISI Workbook Chapter 6 Section 3

6. **A** — A call option is the right to buy at a predetermined price, not the prevailing price

   BPP Study Text Chapter 3 Sections 3.2 and 3.3 / CISI Workbook Chapter 6 Section 3

7. **C** — Futures create obligations on both the part of the buyer and seller

   BPP Study Text Chapter 3 Section 2.1 / CISI Workbook Chapter 6 Section 2

8. **B** — Long call – the risk is limited to the loss of the premium. Long future and short put – the risk is large but limited. Short future – the risk is unlimited

   BPP Study Text Chapter 3 Section 4 / CISI Workbook Chapter 6 Section 2 and 3

9. **A** — The price paid for an option is known as the premium on the option

   BPP Study Text Chapter 3 Section 3.2 / CISI Workbook Chapter 6 Section 3

10. **C** — A call is the right, but not the obligation, of the holder to purchase the underlying at a price agreed at the outset

    BPP Study Text Chapter 3 Section 3.2 / CISI Workbook Chapter 6 Section 3

11. **C** — The writer of a put option has the obligation to buy the underlying if the holder exercises the option. This is better described as a potential obligation

    BPP Study Text Chapter 3 Section 3.3 / CISI Workbook Chapter 6 Section 3

12. **C** — The premium offsets the loss against the exercise price

    BPP Study Text Chapter 3 Section 3.3.4 / CISI Workbook Chapter 6 Section 3

3 ♦ Derivatives – Answers

13. D   The buyer will pay the seller and receive the underlying if the contract goes to delivery

BPP Study Text Chapter 3 Section 2.1 / CISI Workbook Chapter 6 Section 2

14. D   The seller of a call has an unlimited potential loss and the upside is only the premium paid for the option

BPP Study Text Chapter 3 Section 3.2 / CISI Workbook Chapter 6 Section 3

15. B   The writer of an option always has a potential obligation. The holder of an option has a right, but not an obligation

BPP Study Text Chapter 3 Section 3.3.4 / CISI Workbook Chapter 6 Section 3

16. A   The writer faces potentially unlimited losses

BPP Study Text Chapter 3 Section 3.2 / CISI Workbook Chapter 6 Section 3

17. A   A futures contract is exchange-traded and has a fixed price and expiry date

BPP Study Text Chapter 3 Section 1 / CISI Workbook Chapter 6 Section 2

18. B   Only buyers of options must pay the premium

BPP Study Text Chapter 3 Section 3.2 / CISI Workbook Chapter 6 Section 3

19. B   In the case of CDSs, the seller of the protection will pay compensation when a specified credit event occurs, and at that time periodic payments by the protection buyer will also cease to be payable

BPP Study Text Chapter 3 Section 5.2 / CISI Workbook Chapter 6 Section 4

20. A   The seller of protection is prepared to take on additional credit risk, in exchange for income

BPP Study Text Chapter 3 Section 5.2 / CISI Workbook Chapter 6 Section 4.3

4. Financial Product Types

Questions

1. Richard raises a mortgage of £24,000 from a friend. The loan is interest-free and will be repaid at £400 per month. Richard wishes to ensure that his friend is repaid in the event of his own death. What type of life assurance policy would be the most relevant and cost-effective for Richard?

   A Decreasing term
   B Increasing term
   C Endowment
   D Whole of life

2. Eva wishes to provide £50,000 for his dependants in the event of his death. Which type of life assurance policy would be the least expensive to achieve this objective?

   A Term assurance
   B Whole life assurance
   C Endowment
   D Family income benefit

3. A company pension scheme under which participants receive a pension on retirement based on their final salary is called a

   A Deferred benefits scheme
   B Defined benefits scheme
   C Deferred contribution scheme
   D Defined contribution scheme

4. Which of the following is not a common characteristic of the property market?

   A Heterogeneous
   B Indivisible
   C Liquid
   D Decentralised

5. The purpose of liability insurance is to cover

   A Businesses against claims by creditors
   B Mortgage or other loan repayments in the event of unemployment
   C Claims by third parties against the insured
   D Bondholders against the risk of default by the issuer

6. **Which of the following is not one of the features of offshore investment bonds?**

    A The underlying life funds suffer little or no tax

    B Charges are low, making offshore bonds especially appropriate for a short-term holding period

    C Withdrawals of up to 5% of the original investment may be taken for 20 years without an immediate tax liability

    D Offices issuing the bonds are situated in locations that include the Channel Islands, Isle of Man, Dublin and Luxembourg

7. **Assuming the same interest rates, which types of mortgage will have the lowest total of interest payments over a 25-year duration?**

    A Low-cost endowment mortgage

    B Pension-linked mortgage

    C Repayment mortgage

    D ISA-linked mortgage

8. **What is the rule with respect to maximum charges applied by managers for new stakeholder pension plans?**

    A 1.5% for the first 10 years; 1.0% thereafter

    B 1.5% for the first 5 years; 1.0% thereafter

    C 1% for the first 10 years; 0.5% thereafter

    D 1% for the first 5 years; 0.5% thereafter

9. **What is meant by 'the life assured' in respect of a life policy?**

    A The person who pays the premiums

    B The person who benefits from the policy

    C The person whose death will lead to the policy paying out

    D None of the above

10. **Which best describes term assurance?**

    A Cover against loss of earnings over a defined number of years

    B Any life policy with a surrender value

    C A ten-year savings-linked policy

    D Cover against the possibility of death during a specified period

11. **Do term assurance policies have a surrender value?**

    A Yes, in all cases

    B No, in all cases

    C No, except in the case of level term policies

    D Yes, but only in the first 14 days

12. **In what ways are pensions tax-efficient?**

    I   Pension contributions are generally tax-deductible
    II Pension payments out are generally tax-deductible
    III Pension funds do not generally pay tax
    IV Pension payments are taxed at 20% for all recipients

    A I, II and III only
    B II and IV only
    C I and III only
    D I and IV only

13. **What is the tax treatment in respect of receipt of pension payments?**

    A Tax-free in respect of both lump sum and pension
    B Lump sum and pension are both taxable
    C Only the lump sum element is taxed
    D Only the annual payment is taxed

14. **Which of the following incurs the lowest overall interest?**

    A Endowment mortgage
    B Low cost endowment mortgage
    C Deferred interest mortgage
    D Repayment mortgage

15. **Which will get no tax relief on a contribution they make to a registered pension scheme?**

    A Client 1, who is a non-taxpayer aged 19
    B Client 2, who is a basic rate taxpayer aged 77
    C Client 3, who is an additional rate taxpayer aged 42
    D Client 4, who has another personal pension plan for which tax relief is being obtained on contributions in this tax year and is aged 59

16. **Brian would like to invest 'indirectly' in property. Which one of the following would not be a means to do this?**

    A Property bonds
    B REITs
    C Money market fund
    D Unit trusts

17. **For a defined benefits occupational scheme**
    A The benefits must increase in line with the RPI
    B The benefits must increase in line with an average earnings index
    C The benefits are normally based on average earnings close to retirement
    D The benefits normally rise with average earnings over working life

18. **How much of an individual's pension fund held in a registered scheme can normally be taken as a tax-free lump sum?**
    A 15%
    B 20%
    C 25%
    D Nil

19. **A borrower is quoted an interest rate of 12%, charged semi-annually. What is the annual effective rate (AER)?**
    A 11.36%
    B 13.36%
    C 12.36%
    D 14.36%

20. **What does 'AER' stand for?**
    A Annual Equivalent Rate
    B Exponential Average Rate
    C Extra Accrued Rights
    D Endowment Annual Return

21. **Carlos has annual earnings of £175,000. On what level of contributions to a stakeholder pension plan can he get tax relief in 2013/14? Carlos has no annual allowance to carry forward from previous years.**
    A £3,600
    B £50,000
    C £150,000
    D £175,000

22. **A woman earned £12,000 in the current fiscal year. She received interest of £1,000 per month from a building society. At what rate is this interest taxed?**
    A 18%
    B 20%
    C 32½%
    D 40%

23. **Which of the following can term assurance not be used for?**

    A To protect the amount outstanding on a repayment mortgage
    B To provide a lump sum on death if it occurs by a specified date
    C To protect a spouse against the death of the policyholder, whenever this should occur
    D To protect any children until they are 18

24. **An investor who is a basic rate taxpayer deposits £10,000 into an interest-bearing account for three years. If simple interest is paid annually at a rate of 4.5%, how much net interest will the investor receive from the bank in the three-year period?**

    A £450
    B £1,080
    C £1,215
    D £1,350

25. **Which of the following does not describe a type of term life assurance?**

    A With profits
    B Decreasing
    C Level
    D Increasing

26. **Auto-enrolment means that employees will automatically be enrolled in**

    A NEST
    B Either their employer's qualifying pension scheme or NEST
    C Their employer's qualifying pension scheme
    D A stakeholder pension plan

27. **With regard to State pensions, which of the following is not true?**

    A Someone paying National Insurance contributions for 10 years and reaching State Pension age during 2013/14 will receive 50% of the full State pension
    B Someone paying National Insurance contributions for 30 years and reaching State Pension age during 2013/14 will receive a full State pension
    C Pension payments are made gross, but are taxable
    D The State pension age for men is currently 65

28. **What would you normally expect the interest rate on a secured loan to be, compared with an unsecured loan for the same amount and for the same borrower?**

    A Higher
    B The same
    C Lower
    D Impossible to say

4 ♦ Financial Product Types – Questions

29. Which of the following types of mortgage would not be correctly described as an interest-only mortgage?

- A Endowment
- B Pension
- C ISA
- D Repayment

30. A life policy is a contract between

- A Underwriter and investment manager
- B Individual and investment manager
- C Individual and insurance company
- D Investment manager and insurance company

31. If you have a pension-linked mortgage, how much of the final fund will normally be available to repay the loan?

- A 25%
- B 33.3%
- C 20%
- D 35%

32. An occupational money purchase scheme can be described as

- A Defined contributions
- B Defined benefits
- C Additional voluntary contributions
- D Contributory scheme

33. Mr Wong is a 40% (higher rate) taxpayer who lives in the UK. He deposits £10,000 in a building society. How will he be taxed on his earned interest?

- A Nil at source, 40% via his tax return
- B 20% at source, 20% via his tax return
- C 40% at source
- D None of the above

34. In a high interest rate environment, a bank advertises a loan at 12% per annum, with interest charged quarterly. What is the effective annual rate?

- A 12%
- B 12.55%
- C 16.99%
- D 12.3%

35. A credit card company is quoting an annual interest rate of 18%, charged monthly. What is the annual effective rate?

   A   18.5%
   B   19.25%
   C   19.56%
   D   20.5%

36. A borrower is quoted an interest rate of 8%, charged quarterly. What is the annual effective rate (AER)?

   A   8.00%
   B   8.24%
   C   8.50%
   D   9.24%

37. A borrower is quoted an interest rate of 9%, charged semi-annually. What is the annual effective rate (AER)?

   A   8.20%
   B   9.20%
   C   10.20%
   D   11.20%

38. A borrower is quoted an interest rate of 10%, charged quarterly. What is the annual effective rate (AER)?

   A   10.40%
   B   9.40%
   C   11.40%
   D   10.00%

39. A protection policy states: 'Disability means that the insured is totally unable to follow his occupation as stated in the policy and is not following any other occupation.' The policy is most likely to be

   A   Critical illness insurance
   B   Level term assurance
   C   Long-term care insurance
   D   Income protection insurance

40. Which of the following will not normally be covered by a critical illness policy?

   A   Heart attack
   B   Acquired Immune Deficiency Syndrome
   C   Cancer
   D   Stroke

Answers

1. **A** The capital outstanding is decreasing by £400 per month, so a decreasing term policy would be the cheapest and most relevant type of insurance for Richard to take out on his life

   BPP Study Text Chapter 4 Section 7 / CISI Workbook Chapter 10 Section 3.1.2

2. **A** Term assurance would be the cheapest, as this is designed to provide a lump sum and has no investment content. Family income benefit would not be suitable for this purpose, as the sum assured decreases during the term of the cover but provides a constant annual benefit

   BPP Study Text Chapter 4 Section 7 / CISI Workbook Chapter 10 Section 3.1

3. **B** An alternative name for a final salary type scheme is a defined benefit scheme

   BPP Study Text Chapter 4 Section 3.3.1 / CISI Workbook Chapter 9 Section 4.4

4. **C** It might take sometime to sell a property so it is normally described as being an illiquid market

   BPP Study Text Chapter 4 Section 2.1 / CISI Workbook Chapter 3 Section 4

5. **C** Third party liability insurance for individuals is normally included in household insurance policies. Businesses may arrange special liability insurance cover, for example against product liability claims

   BPP Study Text Chapter 4 Section 7.2.6 and 7.2.10 / CISI Workbook Chapter 10 Section 3

6. **B** Charges are relatively high and would typically involve a substantial sacrifice of capital if the holding period is only short

   BPP Study Text Chapter 4 Section 4.2 / CISI Workbook Chapter 9 Section 5

7. **C** A, B and D will have interest payments than C because they are all interest-only type mortgages. With a repayment mortgage, the capital is being repaid and so the interest charged will be decreasing over the term of the mortgage

   BPP Study Text Chapter 4 Section 6 / CISI Workbook Chapter 10 Section 2.4

8. **A** For new plans, charges are limited to 1.5% of the fund value pa for the first ten years and 1% pa thereafter. For plans started before April 2005, a limit of 1% applies in all years

   BPP Study Text Chapter 4 Section 3.6 / CISI Workbook Chapter 9 Section 4.6

9. **C** The life assured is the person whose death will lead to the payout on the policy

   BPP Study Text Chapter 4 Section 7 / CISI Workbook Chapter 10 Section 3.1

10. **D** Term assurance is a contract with an insurer which covers the risk of death over a specified term. There is no surrender value in the contract

    BPP Study Text Chapter 4 Section 7 / CISI Workbook Chapter 10 Section 3.1.2

11. **B** There is no surrender value with term assurance

    BPP Study Text Chapter 4 Section 7 / CISI Workbook Chapter 10 Section 3.1.2

4 ◆ Financial Product Types – Answers

12. **C** Pension contributions within annual allowances are tax-deductible for employee and employer. Pension funds do not generally pay tax. Although the tax credit on UK dividends has been lost, there are no other taxes due within the fund

    BPP Study Text Chapter 4 Section 3.8 / CISI Workbook Chapter 9 Section 4.2

13. **D** The pension payment is taxed as earned income

    BPP Study Text Chapter 4 Section 3.8 / CISI Workbook Chapter 9 Section 4.2

14. **D** Repayment mortgages have the lowest overall level of interest, as capital is being repaid over the term of the mortgage, so the level of interest decreases as capital is repaid

    BPP Study Text Chapter 4 Section 6 / CISI Workbook Chapter 10 Section 2.4

15. **B** To receive tax relief, contributions must be made by age 75. A non-taxpayer can receive tax relief on £3,600 in gross contributions

    BPP Study Text Chapter 4 Section 3.8 / CISI Workbook Chapter 9 Section 4

16. **C** A money market fund is not an indirect property investment, but there are property unit trust funds. REITs are Real Estate Investment Trusts

    BPP Study Text Chapter 4 Section 2 / CISI Workbook Chapter 3 Section 4

17. **C** Defined benefits schemes are also known as final salary schemes, so it makes sense that the benefits are based on remuneration close to retirement and service with the employer

    BPP Study Text Chapter 4 Section 3.3.1 / CISI Workbook Chapter 9 Section 4.4

18. **C** 25% may be taken as a tax-free lump sum

    BPP Study Text Chapter 4 Section 3.5 / CISI Workbook Chapter 9 Section 4.2

19. **C** Consider a loan of £1,000. At a quoted interest rate of 12% per annum, semi-annual interest of 6% on £1,000 is paid at the end of the first six months, ie £60. The second six-months interest of 6% is paid on £1,060, ie £63.60.

    Adding up the interest paid through the year gives £123.60. Therefore the effective rate is 12.36%.

    Another way to calculate this is as follows.

    12% interest per annum / 2 semi-annual periods = 6% per six-months

    Therefore, $(1+r_1) \times (1+r_2) = 1 + AER$

    Thus, $AER = \{(1 + 0.06) \times (1 + 0.06)\} - 1$

    $= (1.06 \times 1.06) - 1$

    $= 1.1236 - 1$

    $= 0.1236 = 12.36\%$

    BPP Study Text Chapter 4 Section 5.2 / CISI Workbook Chapter 10 Section 1.4

20. **A** AER stands for 'annual equivalent rate'. This rate is alternatively referred to as the as the Annual Effective Rate or the Effective Annual Rate

    BPP Study Text Chapter 4 Section 5.2 / CISI Workbook Chapter 10 Section 1.4

21. **B** The annual allowance is £50,000 for 2013/14

    BPP Study Text Chapter 4 Section 3.7 and 3.8 / CISI Workbook Chapter 9 Section 4

22. **B** Investment income from a building society would be taxed at 20% for an investor who is a basic rate taxpayer

BPP Study Text Chapter 4 Section 1 / CISI Workbook Chapter 9 Section 2.1.1

23. **C** It will only protect against death for the term specified in the policy

BPP Study Text Chapter 4 Section 7 / CISI Workbook Chapter 10 Section 3.1.2

24. **B** The withholding tax on interest is 20%.

£10,000 × 4.5% = £450 per year earned in interest. Thus, over three years, the investor earns £1,350.

Now to adjust for tax: £1,350 × (1 − Tax rate) = £1,350 x 80% = £1,080

BPP Study Text Chapter 4 Section 1 / CISI Workbook Chapter 9 Section 2.1.1

25. **A** 'With profits' may relate to whole of life and endowment policies

BPP Study Text Chapter 4 Section 7 / CISI Workbook Chapter 10 Section 3.1.2

26. **B** 'NEST' stands for the National Employment Savings Trust

BPP Study Text Chapter 4 Section 3.4 / CISI Workbook Chapter 9 Section 4.7

27. **A** In order to receive the full State pension, the individual retiring after 5 April 2010 must have credits for 30 qualifying years. Those with fewer qualifying years will receive one thirtieth of the full amount for each qualifying year

BPP Study Text Chapter 4 Section 3.2 / CISI Workbook Chapter 9 Section 4.3

28. **C** All other things being equal, this is true

BPP Study Text Chapter 4 Section 5.3 / CISI Workbook Chapter 10 Section 1.3

29. **D** A repayment mortgage (sometimes known as capital and interest mortgage) is not a type of interest-only mortgage

BPP Study Text Chapter 4 Section 6.2 / CISI Workbook Chapter 10 Section 2.4

30. **C** The proposer is the person who proposes to enter into a contract of insurance with a life insurance company to insure himself, or another person on whose life he has insurable interest

BPP Study Text Chapter 4 Section 7 / CISI Workbook Chapter 10 Section 3

31. **A** The tax-free cash part of the fund can be used to repay the mortgage

BPP Study Text Chapter 4 Section 6.2 / CISI Workbook Chapter 9 Section 4.2

32. **A** Defined contribution schemes are money purchase arrangements. 'Defined benefit scheme' is another name for a final salary scheme

BPP Study Text Chapter 4 Section 3.3.2 / CISI Workbook Chapter 9 Section 4.4

33. **B** The standard deduction of tax at source is 20%

BPP Study Text Chapter 4 Section 1 / CISI Workbook Chapter 9 Section 2.1.1

4 ♦ Financial Product Types – Answers

34. B If interest is quoted at 12% pa, charged on a quarterly basis then the effective annual rate is calculated as follows:

$$\frac{12\% \text{ per annum}}{4 \text{ quarters}} = 3\% \text{ each quarter}$$

Therefore

$$(1+r_1) \times (1+r_2) \times (1+r_3) \times (1+r_4) = 1 + AER$$

$$AER = [1.03 \times 1.03 \times 1.03 \times 1.03] - 1$$
$$= 1.1255 - 1$$
$$= 0.1255 = 12.55\%$$

BPP Study Text Chapter 4 Section 5.2 / CISI Workbook Chapter 10 Section 1.4

35. C If interest is quoted at 18% pa, but charged monthly, then the AER is calculated as follows.

$$\frac{18\% \text{ per annum}}{12 \text{ months}} = 1.5\% \text{ each month}$$

Therefore

$$(1+r_1) \times (1+r_2) \times (1+r_3) \times (1+r_4) \times (1+r_5) \times (1+r_6) \times (1+r_7) \times (1+r_8) \times (1+r_9) \times (1+r_{10}) \times (1+r_{11}) \times (1+r_{12}) = 1 + AER$$

$$= (1+r)^{12} = 1 + AER$$

$$AER = (1 + 0.015)^{12} - 1$$
$$= 1.1956 - 1$$
$$= 0.1956 = 19.56\%$$

BPP Study Text Chapter 4 Section 5.2 / CISI Workbook Chapter 10 Section 1.4

36. B One way to calculate this is to take a loan of £100. At a quoted interest rate of 8% per annum, quarterly rate interest of 2% on £100 is paid at the end of quarter 1, ie £2. The next quarter interest of 2% is paid on £102, ie £2.04. In quarter 3, interest of 2% is paid on £104.04, ie £2.08. In quarter 4, interest of 2% is paid on £106.12, ie £2.12. Adding up the interest paid through the year gives £8.24. Therefore the effective rate is 8.24%.

Another way to calculate this is as follows.

8% interest per annum / 4 quarters = 2% per quarter

Therefore, $(1+r_1) \times (1+r_2) \times (1+r_3) \times (1+r_4) = 1 + AER$

Thus, AER $= \{(1 + 0.02) \times (1 + 0.02) \times (1 + 0.02) \times (1 + 0.02)\} - 1$
$= (1.02 \times 1.02 \times 1.02 \times 1.02) - 1$
$= 1.0824 - 1$
$= 0.0824 = 8.24\%$

BPP Study Text Chapter 4 Section 5.2 / CISI Workbook Chapter 10 Section 1.4

37. **B** Consider a loan of £100. At a quoted interest rate of 9% per annum, semi-annual interest of 4.5% on £100 is paid at the end of the first six months, ie £4.50. The second six months interest of 4.5% is paid on £104.50, ie £4.70.

Adding up the interest paid through the year gives £9.20. Therefore the effective rate is 9.20%.

Another way to calculate this is as follows.

9% interest per annum / 2 semi-annual periods = 4.5% per six-months

Therefore, $(1+r_1) \times (1+r_2) = 1 + \text{AER}$

Thus, $\text{AER} = \{(1 + 0.045) \times (1 + 0.045)\} - 1$

$= (1.045 \times 1.045) - 1$

$= 1.0920 - 1$

$= 0.0920 = 9.20\%$

BPP Study Text Chapter 4 Section 5.2 / CISI Workbook Chapter 10 Section 1.4

38. **A** Suppose there is a loan of £1,000. At a quoted interest rate of 10% per annum, quarterly rate interest of 2.5% on £1,000 is paid at the end of quarter 1, ie £25. The next quarter interest of 2.5% is paid on £1,025, ie £25.63. In quarter 3, interest of 2.5% is paid on £1,050.63, ie £26.26. In quarter 4, interest of 2.5% is paid on £1,076.89, ie £26.92. Adding up the interest paid through the year gives £103.81. Therefore the effective rate is 10.40%.

Another way to calculate this is as follows.

10% interest per annum / 4 quarters = 2.5% per quarter

Therefore, $(1+r_1) \times (1+r_2) \times (1+r_3) \times (1+r_4) = 1 + \text{AER}$

Thus, $\text{AER} = \{(1 + 0.025) \times (1 + 0.025) \times (1 + 0.025) \times (1 + 0.025)\} - 1$

$= (1.025 \times 1.025 \times 1.025 \times 1.025) - 1$

$= 1.104 - 1$

$= 0.104 = 10.4\%$

BPP Study Text Chapter 4 Section 5.2 / CISI Workbook Chapter 10 Section 1.4

39. **D** This would be a statement typically found in IPI policy documentation: IPI typically only pays out if the insured person has loss of earnings and is unable to work

BPP Study Text Chapter 4 Section 7 / CISI Workbook Chapter 10 Section 3.3.2

40. **B** Virtually all CIC policies cover heart attack, cancer and stroke, but AIDS is generally excluded

BPP Study Text Chapter 4 Section 7.2.2 / CISI Workbook Chapter 10 Section 3.3.1

5. Pooled Investment Funds

Questions

1. Which two of the following are roles of the unit trust manager?

    I   Making investment decisions
    II Buying and selling investments for the fund
    III Auditing the fund
    IV Safeguarding the fund's assets

    A I and III
    B II and IV
    C I and IV
    D I and II

2. Which of the following best describes a unit trust?

    A A savings plan which relies on stock market growth and dividends to achieve capital gains for investors
    B A form of life assurance which involves investing in the stock market with certain tax advantages if the unit investments are held for a specified period of time
    C A listed company which relies on stock market growth and dividends to achieve capital gains
    D A fund which relies on stock market growth and dividends to achieve capital gains for investors

3. What is the main purpose of UCITS status?

    A To allow fund managers to charge more than a 15% spread
    B To allow a unit trust to be marketed throughout Europe
    C To allow geared futures and options funds to be freely marketed to the British public
    D To allow any gains made within the fund to remain tax-free

4. Which of the following best describes an OEIC?

    A A company that is the closed-ended equivalent of a unit trust scheme
    B A trust containing pooled investments
    C A company for collective investments, set up so that it can continually issue and redeem its shares, and in which clients can invest
    D A company with a structure that provides income and capital gains tax-free to retail clients

5. Which one of the following investments will often trade at a discount to the underlying net asset value?

    A Exchange traded fund
    B Investment trust shares
    C Units in a unit trust
    D Exchange traded commodity

5 ♦ Pooled Investment Funds – Questions

6. A collective investment scheme that is a 'NURS' is

A   A UCITS scheme which cannot be marketed to retail investors
B   A scheme that does not apply with all UCITS conditions
C   An approved investment trust regular savings plan
D   Alternatively described as a hedge fund

7. Which one of the following statements is not true?

A   The fund manager for a unit trust must invest in accordance with the criteria laid out in a Trust Deed
B   Investing in a unit trust often allows private investors to gain greater diversification
C   Tracker funds are passively managed funds
D   An investment trust is an investment company with variable capital (ICVC)

8. The price of an investment trust's shares represents the

A   Market price based on supply and demand for the shares
B   Valuation from the previous day, as declared by the managers
C   Underlying net asset value after adjusting for tracking error
D   Underlying net asset value

9. In what type of scheme would you expect it to be most likely to find a fund manager quoting bid and offer prices?

A   Index tracking fund
B   Exchange traded fund
C   Unit trust
D   Investment trust

10. When an investment trust share is at a large discount to NAV, which of the following is true?

A   Future capital growth could be higher than with a direct investment
B   There is a guaranteed level of capital growth
C   There will be no capital growth
D   Capital gain is achieved at the expense of income

11. Which of the following statements regarding investment trusts are true?

    I   Their capital structure is fixed
    II   They are traded on the Stock Exchange
    III They are all companies
    IV They can borrow as long as it is permitted in their constitutional documents

A   I, II, III and IV
B   I, III and IV only
C   II and III only
D   I, II and III only

12. Who is the legal owner of assets in an OEIC?

A Trustee
B Authorised Corporate Director
C Manager
D Depository

13. An investment trust is

A A closed-ended fund public limited company
B An open-ended fund with a trust deed
C A closed-ended fund in which extra units can be issued
D An open-ended fund in which extra units can be issued

14. Which of the following best describes an OEIC?

A The French equivalent term for a UCITS
B An Operational Equity Investment Corporation
C An open-ended company with variable capital
D A company mainly investing in European securities

15. What are trustees of a unit trust not responsible for?

A Marketing the units
B Maintaining a register
C Ensuring the manager obeys the trust deed
D Setting up the scheme

16. What is the 'NAV' of a share?

A Notional asset value ÷ Share price
B (Assets minus liabilities) ÷ Number of shares
C Market capitalisation ÷ Number of shares
D Assets ÷ Share price

17. At what price does a unit trust sell units to investors?

A Bid
B Offer
C Mid
D Creation

5 ♦ Pooled Investment Funds – Questions

18. For what two reasons would a unit trust manager price units on a bid basis?

    I   To encourage sellers
    II   To discourage sellers
    III To encourage buyers
    IV To discourage buyers

A I and IV
B II and III
C I and II
D III and IV

19. Which of the following are true of investment trust companies?

    I   They must be UK-resident
    II   They must distribute at least 90% of their income
    III IT companies are closed-ended collective investment schemes
    IV Income must be derived from shares or securities

A I, II, III and IV
B I, II and III only
C I, III and IV only
D III and IV only

20. An investment trust share price is 40p, while the NAV 36p. In this case, we would say that the IT is trading at a

A Premium of 11.1%
B Discount of 11.1%
C Premium of 10.0%
D Discount of 10.0%

21. Which of the following is not true in respect of Real Estate Investment Trusts (REITs)?

A No one person can hold more than 10% of the shares
B 95% of taxable profits must be distributed to investors
C The REIT withholds basic rate tax on distributed profits
D The REIT must be listed on a Recognised Investment Exchange

22. Which of the following statements is true?

A Investment trusts are legal trusts set up with the sole purpose of investing in the securities of other companies
B The price of investment trust shares are determined by taking the net asset value of the trust and dividing by the number of shares in issue
C Where investment trust shares trade at a discount to asset value, there may be a takeover launched for those shares
D Investment trusts are a particular type of unit trust

23. **Performance fees are typically charged by**

    A Hedge funds
    B Money market funds
    C Open ended investment companies
    D Exchange traded funds

24. **Which of the following is not a feature of Exchange-Traded Funds (ETFs)?**

    A No Stamp Duty Reserve Tax is payable by the purchaser
    B The funds are managed with an active investment strategy
    C A price quote will be available throughout the trading day
    D ETFs are open-ended funds

25. **A fund manager may use the investment strategy of arbitrage in order to**

    A Take advantage of price differentials between markets
    B Ensure that the fund tracks an index closely
    C Maximise the dividend yield of the fund
    D Make gains from pound cost averaging

Answers

1. **D** Option III is the role of the auditor and Option IV is the role of the trustee. Option II is something of a grey area. Although officially it is the responsibility of the trustee, he will often delegate this to the manager. Of the choices available, D is the best

   BPP Study Text Chapter 5 Section 2.1 / CISI Workbook Chapter 7 Section 2

2. **D** Answer B describes an endowment policy and answer C describes an investment trust. D is a better answer than A because you can just make a one-off contribution to a unit trust. It does not have to be part of a regular savings plan

   BPP Study Text Chapter 5 Section 2.1 / CISI Workbook Chapter 7 Section 2

3. **B** UCITS status is not automatic: application must be made to the regulator

   BPP Study Text Chapter 5 Section 2.9 / CISI Workbook Chapter 7 Section 1.5.2

4. **C** An OEIC is a type of ICVC (Investment Company with Variable Capital), which can change its capital structure over time. Thus, like a unit trust, it is open-ended

   BPP Study Text Chapter 5 Section 3.1 / CISI Workbook Chapter 7 Section 3

5. **B** The discount arises because investors access the various companies in which the investment trust invests only indirectly and/or because the quality of management of the investment trust is relatively weak

   BPP Study Text Chapter 5 Section 4.2 / CISI Workbook Chapter 7 Section 5.3

6. **B** A non-UCITS retail scheme (NURS) is a scheme that does not comply with all of the UCITS conditions

   BPP Study Text Chapter 5 Section 2.3 / CISI Workbook Chapter 7 Section 1.5.2

7. **D** Tracker funds are passively, not actively, managed. They aim to replicate a basket consisting of all the shares in an index, eg shares that are in the FTSE 100 index

   BPP Study Text Chapter 5 Section 2 / CISI Workbook Chapter 7 Section 3

8. **A** The price of an investment trust is the market price of its shares, which is determined by the supply and demand of the shares

   BPP Study Text Chapter 5 Section 4.2 / CISI Workbook Chapter 7 Section 5.3

9. **C** Dual pricing has traditionally been used for unit trusts

   BPP Study Text Chapter 5 Section 2.5 / CISI Workbook Chapter 7 Section 4.1

10. **A** The discount will mean that each share will have a potential capital gain, for example if the discount narrows or the trust winds up, because the share is currently priced at less than the assets it represents

    BPP Study Text Chapter 5 Section 4.2 / CISI Workbook Chapter 7 Section 5.3

11. **A** If you got this wrong, then go back to your study material notes and re-read the section on investment trusts

    BPP Study Text Chapter 5 Section 4.1 / CISI Workbook Chapter 7 Section 5

5 ♦ Pooled Investment Funds – Answers

12. D The Depositary acts as legal owner and safeguard of assets in an OEIC. The Authorised Corporate Director manages the investments, trades the securities and prices the shares in the OEIC at net asset value

BPP Study Text Chapter 5 Section 3.2 / CISI Workbook Chapter 7 Section 3

13. A Investment trusts are closed-ended companies, quoted on the London Stock Exchange as public limited companies

BPP Study Text Chapter 5 Section 4.1 / CISI Workbook Chapter 7 Section 5

14. C It is an investment company with variable capital

BPP Study Text Chapter 5 Section 3.1 / CISI Workbook Chapter 7 Section 3

15. A The managers of the unit trust are responsible for the marketing of the fund

BPP Study Text Chapter 5 Section 2.1 / CISI Workbook Chapter 7 Section 2

16. B NAV is the value of assets per share after deducting the liabilities of the company

BPP Study Text Chapter 5 Section 4.2 / CISI Workbook Chapter 7 Section 4.1

17. B The unit trust sells units at the offer price, which is the higher price. (The bid price is lower)

BPP Study Text Chapter 5 Section 2.5 / CISI Workbook Chapter 7 Section 4.1

18. B Bid price is the lowest price at which the unit trust can be sold. This is to discourage people from selling and to make the trust more attractive to buyers

BPP Study Text Chapter 5 Section 2.6 / CISI Workbook Chapter 7 Section 4.1

19. C There is no general requirement to distribute 90% of income

BPP Study Text Chapter 5 Section 4.1 / CISI Workbook Chapter 7 Section 5

20. A The share is at a premium because it is priced above the net asset value of the holding of the trust. 4p ÷ 36p × 100 = 11.1%

BPP Study Text Chapter 5 Section 4.2 / CISI Workbook Chapter 7 Section 5.3

21. B A REIT must distribute a minimum of 90% of profits from letting

BPP Study Text Chapter 5 Section 7.2 / CISI Workbook Chapter 7 Section 6

22. C Investment trusts are companies, not legal trusts or unit trusts. Their price is determined by supply and demand for that share. Investment trust shares do tend to trade at a discount to their net asset value

BPP Study Text Chapter 5 Section 4.1 / CISI Workbook Chapter 7 Section 5

23. A Hedge funds typically charge performance-related fees, sometimes of up to 20%

BPP Study Text Chapter 5 Section 6 / CISI Workbook Chapter 7 Section 9

24. B ETFs track indices and, as passive tracker-style funds, they are relatively low-cost

BPP Study Text Chapter 5 Section 5 / CISI Workbook Chapter 7 Section 7

25. A The arbitrageur seeks to exploit inefficient pricing between markets to make a low-risk profit

BPP Study Text Chapter 5 Section 6.3 / CISI Workbook Chapter 6 Section 1.1

6. Financial Services Regulation and Ethics

Questions

1. According to the Data Protection Act 1998, with whom must persons processing personal data register?

   A   The Financial Conduct Authority
   B   HM Treasury
   C   Competition Commissioner
   D   Information Commissioner

2. Which of the following phrases is not an extract from the CISI Code of Conduct?

   A   'Manage fairly and effectively and to the best of your ability any relevant conflict of interest'
   B   'Attain and actively manage a level of professional competence appropriate to your responsibilities'
   C   'Ensure that activities are carried on with an appropriate level of independence'
   D   'Act with integrity in fulfilling the responsibilities of your appointment'

3. During his induction into his job with a firm, Barry is told of the firm's emphasis on managerial responsibility for ethical behaviour combined with a concern for the law. How might this approach best be described?

   A   Supervision approach
   B   An integrity-based programme
   C   A rules-based programme
   D   Professional enforcement

4. Which one of the following is not a sanction with respect to data protection regulation?

   A   A jail term of two years
   B   A £5,000 fine in the Magistrates' Court
   C   An Enforcement Notice issued by the Information Commissioner
   D   An unlimited fine in the Crown Court

5. Which of the following is not stated in the legislation as one of the FCA's objectives?

   A   promoting effective competition in the interests of consumers
   B   securing an appropriate degree of protection for consumers
   C   Promoting the competence of investment advisers
   D   protecting and enhancing the integrity of the UK financial system

6. **Which of the following is true of regulation of financial services in the UK?**

   A Primary legislation is found in FSMA 2000
   B Primary legislation is found in the UCITS directive
   C The FCA was responsible for drafting primary legislation
   D Financial services in the UK are self-regulating

7. **Which of the following is not a specified grouping of controlled functions for approved persons?**

   A Governing functions
   B Necessary functions
   C Systems and control functions
   D Customer functions

8. **The three typical stages of money laundering are**

   A Placement, layering and integration
   B Placement, churning and integration
   C Switching, layering and assimilation
   D Switching, churning and assimilation

9. **Which of the following best describes market abuse?**

   A A criminal offence
   B A breach of contract
   C A civil offence
   D A form of money laaundering

10. **Under the Money Laundering Regulations 2007, authorised firms are responsible for**

    I   Checking the identity of customers
    II   Checking the source of funds
    III Reporting suspicious customers to the authorities
    IV   Assisting in the arrest of suspects

    A I and II only
    B I, II and III only
    C I, III and IV only
    D II, III and IV only

11. **A private investor may make a claim under the Financial Services Compensation Scheme if he loses money as a result of**

   I   A fraud committed by an authorised person
   II A breach of rules by an authorised person
   III The liquidation of an authorised person

   A I only
   B I and II only
   C I and III only
   D III only

12. **Which of the following is a means of obtaining authorisation to conduct investment business in the UK?**

   A Application to the FCA
   B Application to the SEC
   C Membership of an RIE
   D Application to ICMA

13. **The financial crisis of 2007-2009 especially called into question**

   A Outcomes based regulation
   B Self-regulation
   C Statutory regulation
   D Light touch regulation

14. **Which of the following is responsible for insider dealing legislation?**

   A FCA
   B BIS
   C HMT
   D LSE

15. **Which best describes 'layering' in the context of money laundering?**

   A Buying units in an unregulated fund
   B Disguising the source of money
   C Purchasing derivative financial instruments
   D Making many different payments

16. **Which of the following most appropriately describes the style of regulation introduced by the Financial Services and Markets Act 2000?**

   A Self-regulation
   B Regulation by the consumer
   C Ombudsman-regulated
   D Statutory regulation

17. **Suspected money laundering transactions should usually be reported by a firm to the**
    - A Bank of England
    - B Serious Fraud Office
    - C Stock Exchange
    - D Serious Organised Crime Agency (to become the National Crime Agency)

18. **Which body can remove approval from approved persons?**
    - A Office of Fair Trading
    - B Treasury
    - C Department for Business, Innovation and Skills
    - D Financial Conduct Authority

19. **If an individual has a total claim of £35,000 for investments, what would be the maximum amount of compensation he could receive under the Financial Services Compensation Scheme?**
    - A Nil
    - B £31,500
    - C £35,000
    - D £17,500

20. **In what circumstances does the Financial Services Compensation Scheme pay out?**
    - A When a firm closes down and an investor loses money
    - B When poor advice is given and an investor loses money
    - C When the regulator does not regulate efficiently and an investor loses money
    - D When an investor loses money in any circumstances

21. **For protected investments, the Financial Services Compensation Scheme sets a maximum payout of**
    - A £50,000
    - B £30,000 plus 90% of next £20,000
    - C £45,000 plus 90% of next £40,000
    - D £85,000

22. **The market abuse legislation does not cover trading on**
    - A LSE
    - B ISDX
    - C LIFFE
    - D NYSE

23. **Regarding complaints procedures, which of the following need to be in place?**

    I   Written procedures to handle complaints
    II Advice to the client about where to go if not satisfied
    III An officer in the firm whose sole role is in respect of handling complaints
    IV Review of all complaints by the regulator

    A   I, II, III and IV
    B   I, II and III only
    C   I and II only
    D   I, III and IV only

24. **Which statements are true regarding insider dealing legislation in the Criminal Justice Act 1993?**

    I   Offences may only be committed by an individual, not a company
    II Encouraging a third party to deal on the basis of insider information is an offence
    III UK equities, gilts and related derivatives are all caught by the legislation
    IV Disclosure of price-sensitive information to a third party (other than the normal course of employment) is an offence

    A   I, II and III only
    B   I, II and IV only
    C   II, III and IV only
    D   I, II, III and IV

25. **If a complaint investigated by a firm has not been conciliated, to which of the following can the complaint be referred?**

    A   Office of Fair Trading
    B   Financial Ombudsman Service
    C   Complaints Commissioner
    D   Financial Services Compensation Scheme

26. **The Financial Ombudsman Service was established by**

    A   The FSA (which has become the FCA)
    B   The Bank of England
    C   HMT
    D   The Lord Chancellor

27. **Which one of the following statements about the Financial Ombudsman Service (FOS) is not true?**

    A   The maximum award by the Ombudsman is £150,000 plus costs
    B   The chairman and board of directors of the FOS are appointed by the FCA
    C   The FOS can hear cases regarding non-regulated activities where firms agree to the voluntary jurisdiction of the FOS
    D   The FOS is available to any person, in respect of regulated activities

28. If the outcome of the Financial Ombudsman investigation is declined by the complainant, then it is

A Determined by HM Treasury
B Always determined by the courts
C Binding on the firm
D Not binding on the firm

29. Which of the following is true?

A The maximum payout of the Financial Ombudsman Service is £85,000 plus costs
B The maximum payout of the Financial Services Compensation Scheme is £100,000 per person
C The maximum fine for market abuse is £1,000,000
D The maximum payout of the Financial Ombudsman Service is £150,000 plus costs

30. For market abuse to have occurred

A There must be intention
B There must be intention and effect
C There must be effect
D There need not be effect

31. Which of the following statements about the Joint Money Laundering Steering Group is true?

A It explains, in its guidance notes, how to apply the statutory regulations relating to money laundering
B It is a division of the FCA
C It only applies to non-UK firms passporting into the UK
D It relates to market abuse

32. Which of the following is false in respect of the Money Laundering Regulations?

A Simplified due diligence procedures should be used for politically exposed persons
B The Regulations apply to financial institutions and credit institutions
C Where the client is introduced by an authorised firm, the firm can rely on the introducer for identification
D Firms must take a risk-based approach to money laundering prevention

33. Which of the following is most probably not a possible means of attempting theft of customer data?

A Phishing
B Key loggers
C Card readers fitted to ATMs
D Denial of service (DoS) attack

34. **Which two of the following types of documentation would be appropriate for a firm to use to identify its trust clients for money laundering purposes?**

    I   A passport or driving licence
    II A certificate of incorporation and evidence of the company's registered address
    III A copy of the latest report and accounts
    IV A trust deed

    A III and IV
    B II and III
    C I and IV
    D I and III

35. **Which of the following is an accepted defence against the offence of failure to prevent bribery, under the Bribery Act 2010?**

    A Bribes were paid by persons associated with the firm and not by employees
    B Bribes were acceptable under local customs in a foreign jurisdiction
    C Adequate procedures to prevent bribery were in place
    D The board of directors had no knowledge of the bribery

36. **The principle of integrity is the first Statement of Principle for Approved Persons. Which of the following behaviour is least likely to constitute a breach of this Principle?**

    A Providing false or inaccurate information to the regulator
    B Deliberately aiming to achieve maximum appropriate profits
    C Deliberately failing to disclose the existence of a conflict of interest
    D Misleading others in the firm about the nature of risks being accepted

37. **Which of the following is not one of the Principles for Businesses of the FCA?**

    A Clients' assets
    B Integrity
    C Polarisation
    D Financial prudence

38. **A firm does not have adequate systems for compliance oversight. With which of the FCA Principles for Businesses is it failing to comply?**

    A Customers' interests
    B Financial prudence
    C Management and control
    D Skill, care and diligence

6 ♦ Financial Services Regulation and Ethics – Answers

Answers

1. **D** The Information Commissioner maintains a public registry of data controllers

   BPP Study Text Chapter 6 Section 4 / CISI Workbook Chapter 8 Section 5

2. **C** C should be covered by a firm's conflict of interest policy but is not part of the wording of the CISI Code of Conduct. The words in A, B and D are included in CISI Principles 5, 6 and 2 respectively

   BPP Study Text Chapter 6 Section 6.2 / CISI Workbook Chapter 8 Section 7.6.2

3. **B** An integrity-based approach combines a concern for the law with an emphasis on managerial responsibility for ethical behaviour

   BPP Study Text Chapter 6 Section 7.7.2 / CISI Workbook Chapter 8 Section 7.3

4. **A** Although a breach of DPA 1998 is a criminal offence, there is no option of a jail sentence

   BPP Study Text Chapter 6 Section 4 / CISI Workbook Chapter 8 Section 5

5. **C** Promoting the competence of investment advisers will hopefully follow on from the statutory objectives, but is not itself one of the specified objectives

   BPP Study Text Chapter 6 Section 1.2.2 / CISI Workbook Chapter 8 Section 1.2.1

6. **A** FSMA 2000 was drafted by HM Treasury and is enforced by the FCA

   BPP Study Text Chapter 6 Section 1 / CISI Workbook Chapter 8 Section 1.2.1

7. **B** The correct wording is 'required functions'

   BPP Study Text Chapter 6 Section 1.6 / CISI Workbook Chapter 8 Section 1.4

8. **A** Placement involves getting the dirty cash into the system initially, layering involves many transactions in an attempt to disguise its true origins, and integration is the process during which the clean funds are re-entered into the system

   BPP Study Text Chapter 6 Section 2.2 / CISI Workbook Chapter 8 Section 2.1.1

9. **C** Market abuse is a civil offence and as such the person found guilty cannot be imprisoned

   BPP Study Text Chapter 6 Section 3.3 / CISI Workbook Chapter 8 Section 4

10. **B** Money laundering regulation is an important topic.

    I   True – It is a requirement that institutions have procedures for checking the identity of clients

    II True – The institution may need to enquire as to the source of funds

    III True – Reporting suspicions is an important part of the legislation

    IV False – You are not expected to assist the police in the arrest of the suspect

    BPP Study Text Chapter 6 Section 2.8 / CISI Workbook Chapter 8 Section 2.1

11. **D** Compensation is paid by the FSCS where the company concerned is or is likely to become insolvent

    BPP Study Text Chapter 6 Section 5.3 / CISI Workbook Chapter 8 Section 6.4

6 ♦ Financial Services Regulation and Ethics – Answers

12. **A** The SEC is a regulator in the US. While RIEs are exempt, membership alone is not a 'means of obtaining authorisation'. ICMA regulates the Eurobond market

    BPP Study Text Chapter 6 Section 1.4 / CISI Workbook Chapter 8 Section 1.3

13. **D** 'Light touch' regulation is the best answer. The financial services regulator responded by introducing a more 'intrusive' supervisory regime

    BPP Study Text Chapter 6 Section 1.1 / CISI Workbook Chapter 8 Section 7.6

14. **C** The legislation is the responsibility of the Treasury, but the investigation and prosecution of the offence is the responsibility of the Department for Business, Innovation and Skills

    BPP Study Text Chapter 6 Section 3.2 / CISI Workbook Chapter 8 Section 3

15. **B** Layering is one of the stages of the typical money laundering process

    Placement: getting the money into the financial system

    Layering: separating the money from its illegal origin

    Integration: process is complete, the money has been laundered and looks as if it has come from a legitimate source

    BPP Study Text Chapter 6 Section 2.2 / CISI Workbook Chapter 8 Section 2.1.1

16. **D** The FSMA 2000 introduced a system of statutory regulation – moving away from the earlier 'self-regulation within a statutory framework'

    BPP Study Text Chapter 6 Section 1.1 / CISI Workbook Chapter 8 Section 1.2.1

17. **D** The Serious Organised Crime Agency (SOCA) – to become the National Crime Agency – is the government body that co-ordinates money laundering enquiries

    BPP Study Text Chapter 6 Section 2.5.1 / CISI Workbook Chapter 8 Section 2.1.3

18. **D** The regulator can remove approval from approved persons

    BPP Study Text Chapter 6 Section 1.6 / CISI Workbook Chapter 8 Section 1.3

19. **C** The maximum amount the FSCS pays in relation to protected investments is 100% of the first £50,000

    BPP Study Text Chapter 6 Section 5.3 / CISI Workbook Chapter 8 Section 6.4

20. **A** The Financial Services Compensation Scheme pays out when the firm becomes insolvent or is likely to become insolvent

    BPP Study Text Chapter 6 Section 5.3 / CISI Workbook Chapter 8 Section 6.4

21. **A** The maximum FSCS compensation for protected investments is £50,000

    BPP Study Text Chapter 6 Section 5.3 / CISI Workbook Chapter 8 Section 6.4

22. **D** The offence of market abuse covers UK markets and the main EEA exchanges

    BPP Study Text Chapter 6 Section 3.3 / CISI Workbook Chapter 8 Section 4

6 ♦ Financial Services Regulation and Ethics – Answers

23. **C** There needs to be a written procedure on how to handle complaints, and the client must be informed on the next stage of the complaints procedure if they are not satisfied. Complaints need to be handled by a sufficiently senior person

    BPP Study Text Chapter 6 Section 5.1 / CISI Workbook Chapter 8 Section 6.1

24. **D** All of the options are correct. Be aware of the legislation regarding insider dealing and the defences that can be used

    BPP Study Text Chapter 6 Section 3.2 / CISI Workbook Chapter 8 Section 3

25. **B** The Complaints Commissioner investigates individual complaints against the regulators themselves

    BPP Study Text Chapter 6 Section 5.2 / CISI Workbook Chapter 8 Section 6.3

26. **A** Established by, but independent from, the regulator

    BPP Study Text Chapter 6 Section 5.2 / CISI Workbook Chapter 8 Section 6.3

27. **D** The service is available to 'eligible complainants'

    BPP Study Text Chapter 6 Section 5.2 / CISI Workbook Chapter 8 Section 6.3

28. **D** If the complaining customers refuses to accept the outcome of the FOS investigation, then it is not binding on the firm. Instead, the complainant may choose to take or not to take their case to courts

    BPP Study Text Chapter 6 Section 5.2 / CISI Workbook Chapter 8 Section 6.3

29. **D** The maximum payout by the Ombudsman is currently £150,000 plus costs

    BPP Study Text Chapter 6 Section 5.2 / CISI Workbook Chapter 8 Section 6.3

30. **C** It is possible to have abused a market without intention to do so through, for example, negligence. The legislation is effect-based

    BPP Study Text Chapter 6 Section 3.3 / CISI Workbook Chapter 8 Section 4

31. **A** The guidance notes are just that: they are there for guidance. The JMLSG is not part of the FCA

    BPP Study Text Chapter 6 Section 2.3 / CISI Workbook Chapter 8 Section 2.1.3

32. **A** It is permissible for one authorised firm to rely on the written assurance of another authorised firm for money laundering identification purposes. The position of PEPs can make them vulnerable to corruption, and enhanced due diligence is therefore appropriate

    BPP Study Text Chapter 6 Section 2.8 / CISI Workbook Chapter 8 Section 2.1

33. **D** A denial-of-service attack is an attempt to make a computer or network resource unavailable to its intended users. Phishing, key loggers and card readers are all methods used by criminals to steal customer data

    BPP Study Text Chapter 6 Section 2.10 / CISI Workbook Chapter 8 Section 2.3

34. **A** A passport or driving licence would help identify an individual and a certificate of incorporation would identify a corporate client only and not a trust client

    BPP Study Text Chapter 6 Section 2.8 / CISI Workbook Chapter 8 Section 2.3

35. **C** That adequate procedures were in place is a defence

    BPP Study Text Chapter 6 Section 2.9 / CISI Workbook Chapter 8 Section 2.2

36. **B** Aiming to maximise profits seems to be a normal business aim rather than a breach of the principle of integrity

    BPP Study Text Chapter 6 Section 7.8 / CISI Workbook Chapter 8 Section 7

37. **C** Polarisation, an advice-giving regime abolished in 2005, is not one of the eleven Principles for Businesses

    BPP Study Text Chapter 6, Sections 1.5 / CISI Workbook Chapter 8 Section 1.3

38. **C** The management and control principle requires firms to have adequate risk management systems, which would include adequate systems for compliance oversight

    BPP Study Text Chapter 6, Sections 1.5 / CISI Workbook Chapter 8 Section 1.3

7. Tax, ISAs and Trusts

Questions

1. Which one of the following is not a chargeable disposal for capital gains tax purposes?

    A   Sale of gilts
    B   Sale of property
    C   Gift of shares to one's brother
    D   Sale of shares to a company pursuant to a share repurchase scheme approved by the shareholders in general meeting

2. From and to which dates does the fiscal year run?

    A   1 April to 31 March
    B   5 April to 6 April
    C   6 April to 5 April
    D   5 April to 5 April

3. CGT is not levied on

    A   Sale of shares
    B   Sale of gilts
    C   Sale of second home
    D   Sale of futures

4. Which of the following transfers is exempt from inheritance tax?

    A   Gift to a civil partner
    B   Gift to children
    C   Gift made one month before death
    D   Gifts between siblings

5. Which tax regime makes it advantageous to give away your assets prior to your death?

    A   Capital gains tax
    B   Inheritance tax
    C   Stamp duty
    D   Income tax

6. Which of the following are not exempt from CGT?

    A   Gilts
    B   An individual's main residence
    C   Antiques
    D   Wasting assets

7. **Bank deposit account interest is normally paid after tax deducted at source of**

   A 10%
   B 20%
   C 32½%
   D 40%

8. **What is an individual's annual exemption for capital gains tax purposes, for the fiscal year 2013/14?**

   A £9,440
   B £10,600
   C £10,900
   D £325,000

9. **Which of the following allowances/exemptions can be carried forward one year?**

   A Personal allowance under income tax
   B Annual exempt allowance for capital gains tax purposes
   C Inheritance tax annual gifts exemption
   D Inheritance tax exemption for marriage gifts

10. **A widower makes a gift of £100,000 to each of his two children. This is a 'potentially exempt transfer'. How long must he live for there to be no tax payable in respect of these transfers?**

    A Three years
    B Five years
    C Seven years
    D Nine years

11. **What is the maximum gift without Inheritance Tax implications that a parent can make in consideration of the marriage of a daughter?**

    A £1,000
    B £2,500
    C £5,000
    D £10,000

12. **What additional liability to income tax exists for an individual in respect of UK dividends where the cash amount of dividend received was £600 and total other earnings are £19,600?**

    A Nil
    B £60
    C £67
    D £150

13. **What leads to a capital gains tax liability?**

    A Chargeable purchase of a chargeable asset by a chargeable person

    B Increase in value of a chargeable asset that is owned by a chargeable person

    C Chargeable disposal of a chargeable asset by a chargeable person

    D A revision to the inflation figure in a year when a capital gain is made

14. **Paul has made a loss on selling shares of £5,000. For how long can he carry this loss forward for offset in the future?**

    A Six months

    B Two years

    C Six years

    D Indefinite

15. **On which of the following are losses on disposal not allowable for capital gains tax purposes?**

    A Gilts

    B Traded options

    C Financial futures

    D A holiday home in Florida

16. **Farid transfers a holding of shares to his wife. Which of the following is true?**

    A Capital gains tax is payable by Farid on this transfer

    B Capital gains tax is payable by Farid's wife on this transfer

    C No tax is payable currently, since this is a potentially exempt transfer between husband and wife

    D No tax is payable currently, but Farid's wife is deemed to have acquired the shares at the original cost to Farid

17. **From the following list, which will be taxed as earned income?**

    A Taxable benefits in kind

    B Building Society interest

    C Dividend income

    D Income from land or property

18. **A man transferred £500,000 to his wife (who is UK-domiciled) and then died three years later. When is inheritance tax payable, if any, on the amount transferred?**

    A Immediately

    B When the wife dies

    C No tax is payable

    D After four more years from date of death

19. In 2013/14, Jamal earns £24,000 per annum. In the same year, she receives £1,000 gross income from a building society and £1,000 in dividends. How much extra income tax, if any, does she have to pay on the dividends?

    A £nil
    B £111
    C £361
    D £525

20. If Devraj makes a gift of £7,000 to his ex-wife Hamsa, what time period must have elapsed between the gift and his death so that it is not taxable?

    A None
    B One year
    C Five years
    D Seven years

21. If Mr and Mrs Lefevre have not used up their inheritance tax gift exemption for last year, what is the most they can give as a gift in 2013/14 between them, utilising only the IHT annual exemption?

    A £3,000
    B £6,000
    C £9,000
    D £12,000

22. How many gifts can be made to different individuals, of £250 per individual, by one individual in one year without incurring an inheritance tax liability?

    A 12
    B 24
    C 32
    D There is no limit

23. The VAT rate is 0% on all of the following, except

    A Newspapers
    B Children's clothes
    C Electrical goods
    D Food bought in a supermarket

24. Which of the following is not a participant in a trust?

    A Depositary
    B Settlor
    C Beneficiary
    D Trustee

7 ♦ Tax, ISAs and Trusts – Questions

25. **The Renshaw No.1 Trust is a discretionary trust. Who has the task of deciding who should receive income payments and when?**

    A   The trustee
    B   The settlor
    C   The beneficiary
    D   The life tenant

26. **A trust is established with a sole beneficiary. The beneficiary of the trust has the absolute and immediate right to both the income and capital from the trust. This form of trust is best described as a**

    A   Bare trust
    B   Lifetime trust
    C   Charitable trust
    D   Discretionary trust

27. **Which of the following statements is true?**

    A   Stamp duty reserve tax is chargeable on a transfer of certificated shares
    B   Stamp duty reserve tax chargeable is rounded up to the nearest £5
    C   When chargeable, stamp duty is payable by the purchaser in a transaction
    D   Stamp duty is charged at a rate of 1%, subject to rounding

28. **An ISA can be described as**

    A   A tax-efficient savings scheme
    B   A collective investment scheme
    C   A company investing in another company
    D   A type of personal pension plan

29. **Which one of the following statements is true with regard to ISAs, in respect of 2013/14?**

    A   The maximum that an investor aged 58 can invest in a cash ISA is £3,600
    B   Income and capital gains are tax-free
    C   The maximum overall investment for a person aged 60 is £15,000
    D   An investor cannot open both a stocks and shares ISA and a cash ISA with different providers in the same tax year

30. **Which of the following sequences of transactions is not possible within ISA rules, in a newly opened cash ISA, if all transactions occur in the current tax year?**

    A   £3,000 deposit; £1,000 withdrawal; £2,000 deposit
    B   £1,500 deposit; £800 withdrawal; £500 withdrawal; £2,000 deposit
    C   £1,500 deposit; £3,500 deposit; £200 withdrawal
    D   £3,000 deposit; £3,000 withdrawal; £3,000 deposit

31. **What is the maximum payable into a cash ISA by Mr Chakravarti, aged 34, in the current tax year?**

    A £11,520
    B £5,760
    C £3,600
    D £7,200

32. **Which of the following is true of a stocks and shares ISA?**

    A The maximum contribution is reduced if the individual pays into their cash ISA during the same tax year
    B Civil partners or spouses can hold a joint ISA
    C Capital gains tax is levied when the total account value exceeds £1 million
    D There is no limit on the total account value

33. **How much can Paul and Barry, who are civil partners, invest in total in ISAs that are in their names during the fiscal year 2013/14?**

    A £7,200
    B £11,280
    C £20,400
    D £22,560

34. **Of the following dates, which indicate a time period within which two stocks and shares ISAs could be started by a single individual?**

    A 6 April 2013 to 6 December 2013 inclusive
    B 1 April 2013 to 5 March 2014 inclusive
    C 30 June 2013 to 31 January 2014 inclusive
    D 31 December 2013 to 5 April 2014 inclusive

35. **If a 45-year old individual invests £1,500 into a cash ISA in December 2013, what is the maximum investment she can make into the same cash ISA in the March 2014? She makes no other ISA investments.**

    A £11,520
    B £10,020
    C £5,760
    D £4,260

36. **Which of the following is not correct regarding ISA transfers?**

    A   The investor can transfer part or all of their cash ISAs from previous tax years into stocks and shares ISAs, with their present or another provider, without affecting their current annual ISA investment allowance

    B   The investor can transfer all (but not only part of) the money saved so far in a current tax year cash ISA into a stocks and shares ISA, with their present or another provider

    C   After the first year, the investor may transfer an ISA to a different manager, in which case all assets and financial instruments in the ISA must be transferred

    D   ISA managers are required to allow transfers between managers, although a manager is not required to accept a transfer in

37. **The following statements concern investment wrappers for children. Which is true?**

    A   All Child Trust Funds have become known as Junior ISAs

    B   Junior ISAs are limited to the same investments as the cash ISA and cannot hold stocks and shares

    C   The Junior ISA is managed directly by the child after age 14

    D   The Junior ISA converts to a standard ISA when the child reaches age 18

38. **Gabriel was born on 2 May 2013. Which Individual Savings Accounts (including Junior ISAs (JISAs)) can be opened in his name in the tax year 2013/14?**

    A   None

    B   One cash JISA only

    C   One cash JISA plus one stocks and shares JISA only

    D   One normal cash ISA plus one cash JISA only

Answers

1. **A**   Gilts are exempt from capital gains tax. Answer D may sound complicated, but it is a sale of shares and therefore potentially liable to CGT

   BPP Study Text Chapter 7 Section 2.2 / CISI Workbook Chapter 9 Section 2.2

2. **C**   The fiscal year relates to a year for which a personal tax calculation is performed

   BPP Study Text Chapter 7 Section 1.2 / CISI Workbook Chapter 9 Section 2

3. **B**   Gilts, main home and wasting assets are exempt from CGT

   BPP Study Text Chapter 7 Section 2.2 / CISI Workbook Chapter 9 Section 2.2

4. **A**   Gifts between spouses or civil partners are exempt from IHT

   BPP Study Text Chapter 7 Section 3.3 / CISI Workbook Chapter 9 Section 2.3

5. **B**   Unless assets are gifted seven years or more prior to death, they could be chargeable to IHT

   BPP Study Text Chapter 7 Section 3.2 / CISI Workbook Chapter 9 Section 2.3

6. **C**   Sale of antiques represents a chargeable disposal for purposes of CGT

   BPP Study Text Chapter 7 Section 2.2 / CISI Workbook Chapter 9 Section 2.2

7. **B**   Interest income from bank accounts suffers 20% tax at source, except for income from gilts, which is normally received gross. Non-taxpayers can complete HMRC form R85, which allows bank or building society interest to be paid gross, with no tax withheld at source

   BPP Study Text Chapter 7 Section 1.3 / CISI Workbook Chapter 9 Section 2.1.1

8. **C**   The annual exemption for capital gains tax is separate from the personal allowance for income tax

   BPP Study Text Chapter 7 Section 2.3 / CISI Workbook Chapter 9 Section 2.2

9. **C**   The annual IHT gifts exemption is available to carry forward for one year only

   BPP Study Text Chapter 7 Section 3.5 / CISI Workbook Chapter 9 Section 2.3

10. **C**   There is no tax due on a potentially exempt transfer, once the donor has survived for seven years following the gift

    BPP Study Text Chapter 7 Section 3.2 / CISI Workbook Chapter 9 Section 2.3

11. **C**   Each parent may make a gift of £5,000, which will be exempt on consideration of marriage

    BPP Study Text Chapter 7 Section 3.4 / CISI Workbook Chapter 9 Section 2.3

12. **A**   The individual is a basic rate taxpayer. There is no further liability on dividends for a basic rate taxpayer, as a 10% notional tax credit has been received on the dividend

    BPP Study Text Chapter 7 Section 1.4 / CISI Workbook Chapter 9 Section 2.1.2

7 ◆ Tax, ISAs and Trusts – Answers

13. **C** Capital gains tax is paid on a chargeable disposal if there is not enough unused losses or annual exemption to set off against the gain

    BPP Study Text Chapter 7 Section 2.1 / CISI Workbook Chapter 9 Section 2.2

14. **D** Losses can be carried forward indefinitely for capital gains tax purposes

    BPP Study Text Chapter 7 Section 2.3 / CISI Workbook Chapter 9 Section 2.2

15. **A** Gains on gilts are exempt from CGT and accordingly losses are not allowable

    BPP Study Text Chapter 7 Section 2.2 / CISI Workbook Chapter 9 Section 2.2

16. **D** Transfers between husband and wife are deemed to be no loss/gain transactions

    BPP Study Text Chapter 7 Section 2.2 / CISI Workbook Chapter 9 Section 2.2

17. **A** Taxable benefits in kind are taxed as earned income. Note that income from property is treated as unearned income

    BPP Study Text Chapter 7 Section 1 / CISI Workbook Chapter 9 Section 2.1

18. **C** No tax is payable on the man's death, nor on her death, if the wife's total assets are lower than the combination of her own nil-rate band and that of her husband's. If, at her death, the wife has assets in excess of the combined nil-rate bands, then IHT will be due on that excess. This also assumes that the wife is UK-domiciled – as stated in this question – but you should take this to be the case unless the question states otherwise

    BPP Study Text Chapter 7 Section 3.3 / CISI Workbook Chapter 9 Section 2.3

19. **A** The dividends are received with a 10% tax credit which means that Jamal's liability to basic rate tax is removed: she will have no further tax to pay as long as her total income remains below the higher rate band

    BPP Study Text Chapter 7 Section 1.4 / CISI Workbook Chapter 9 Section 2.1.2

20. **D** As Hamsa is the ex-wife of Devraj, this gift will not benefit from the spouse's transfer exemption. It will be a potentially exempt transfer and requires seven full years to expire before the gift becomes exempt

    BPP Study Text Chapter 7 Section 3.2 / CISI Workbook Chapter 9 Section 2.3

21. **D** The couple will be able to give £6,000 each. £6,000 × 2 = £12,000 and this will use up the annual exemptions. There is no limit on the amount that the couple can give away, but this will be potentially subject to tax

    BPP Study Text Chapter 7 Section 3.5 / CISI Workbook Chapter 9 Section 2.3

22. **D** There is no limit on the number of £250 gifts that may be made

    BPP Study Text Chapter 7 Section 3.4 / CISI Workbook Chapter 9 Section 2.3

23. **C** All of the others are exempt from VAT

    BPP Study Text Chapter 7 Section 6 / CISI Workbook Chapter 9 Section 2.5

24. **A** 'Depositary' is the name used to describe the trustee of an OEIC

    BPP Study Text Chapter 7 Section 8.2 / CISI Workbook Chapter 9 Section 6

7 ♦ Tax, ISAs and Trusts – Answers

25.	A	The trustee is responsible for making this decision

BPP Study Text Chapter 7 Section 8.3 / CISI Workbook Chapter 9 Section 6.3

26.	A	A bare trust is also known as a simple trust. The trustee has no discretion over payment of income or capital to the beneficiary

BPP Study Text Chapter 7 Section 8.3 / CISI Workbook Chapter 9 Section 6.3

27.	C	For certificated shares, stamp duty is chargeable, not SDRT. SDRT is rounded up to the nearest 1p. Stamp duty is charged at 0.5%, rounded up to the nearest £5. Stamp duty or SDRT are payable, as applicable, by the purchaser in the transaction

BPP Study Text Chapter 7 Section 5 / CISI Workbook Chapter 9 Section 2.4

28.	A	Both income and capital gains are free from tax within an ISA

BPP Study Text Chapter 7 Section 7.1 / CISI Workbook Chapter 9 Section 3

29.	B	For an individual aged 18 or over, the maximum investment (2013/14) is £11,520, of which £5,760 may be invested in a cash ISA

BPP Study Text Chapter 7 Section 7.2 / CISI Workbook Chapter 9 Section 3.1.4

30.	D	Under choice A, a total of £5,000 has been deposited. For B, £3,500 has been deposited. Under choice C, £5,000 has been deposited. Choice D breaks the rules as it involves a total of £6,000 in deposits in the same tax year

BPP Study Text Chapter 7 Section 7.2 / CISI Workbook Chapter 9 Section 3.1.4

31.	B	£5,760 may be paid into a cash ISA in the tax year 2013/14

BPP Study Text Chapter 7 Section 7.2 / CISI Workbook Chapter 9 Section 3

32.	A	An ISA cannot be held jointly by two people (Option B). There is no restriction relating to the overall value of an ISA (Options C and D). It is not possible for anyone under 18 to purchase an ISA. (However, over-16s can open and contribute to a cash ISA)

BPP Study Text Chapter 7 Section 7.1 / CISI Workbook Chapter 9 Section 3

33.	D	The annual limit for ISAs is £11,520 per person (2013/14). Therefore the total they can invest would be £23,040

BPP Study Text Chapter 7 Section 7.2 / CISI Workbook Chapter 9 Section 3

34.	B	These dates span two tax years, so two stocks and shares ISAs may be started

BPP Study Text Chapter 7 Section 7.1 / CISI Workbook Chapter 9 Section 3

35.	D	£5,760 minus £1,500 leaves £4,260 for investment in the cash ISA

BPP Study Text Chapter 7 Section 7.2 / CISI Workbook Chapter 9 Section 3

36.	C	C being incorrect, the correct position is as follows. The investor may transfer an ISA to a different manager in the year of subscription, in which case the entire ISA subscription for that year must be transferred. After the first year however, partial (or full) transfers between ISA managers are permitted

BPP Study Text Chapter 7 Section 7.3 / CISI Workbook Chapter 9 Section 3

37. **D** CTFs exist alongside Junior ISAs, but a child cannot have both types of account: if eligible for a CTF, the child cannot also open a JISA. A Junior ISA may be a cash account, or a stocks and shares account. A child may become the registered contact for their JISA after age 16

    BPP Study Text Chapter 7 Section 7.4 / CISI Workbook Chapter 9 Section 3.2

38. **C** Each type of JISA can be opened for the child, but not a normal (non-Junior) cash ISA

    BPP Study Text Chapter 7 Section 7.4 / CISI Workbook Chapter 9 Section 3.2

Practice Examinations

Contents

Practice Examinations	Page Number	
	Questions	Answers
Practice Examination 1	79	89
Practice Examination 2	93	103
Practice Examination 3	109	119
Practice Examination 4	123	133
Practice Examination 5	137	147

Practice Examination 1

50 Questions in 1 Hour

1. **Which of the following are primarily the clients of the retail sector?**

   A Personal and institutional investors
   B Institutional investors
   C Commercial businesses
   D Personal investors

2. **Which of the following has responsibility for looking after investments on behalf of fund managers, pension funds and insurance companies?**

   A Trustee
   B Registrar
   C Depository
   D Custodian

3. **Which of the following sets interest rates in the UK?**

   A Prudential Regulation Authority
   B Governor of the Bank of England
   C HM Treasury
   D Monetary Policy Committee

4. **Creation of credit occurs due to**

   A Issuance of notes and coins into the economy
   B Bank lending
   C Increase in inflation
   D Increasing exports

5. **Which of the following is most likely to benefit from inflation?**

   A Savers
   B Borrowers
   C Exporters
   D Retired pensioners

6. **What will be the effect on the interest paid to an investor, if form R85 is completed and accepted?**

   A   Interest will be credited monthly
   B   The rate of interest credited will reduce
   C   Interest will be credited annually
   D   Interest will be paid gross with no deduction of tax

7. **An investor who pays tax at 40% invests £20,000 in a bank. £3,000 of this is placed in a Cash ISA and the remaining sum in a high interest account. Both pay interest at a rate of 4.5% gross. What will be the monetary sum received at the end of the year?**

   A   £540
   B   £594
   C   £747
   D   £900

8. **How often are Treasury Bill tenders held?**

   A   Daily
   B   Weekly
   C   Monthly
   D   Annually

9. **What is the interest on a bond known as?**

   A   Yield
   B   Dividend
   C   Coupon
   D   Debenture

10. **In which of the following types of property investment is a small investor with a diversified portfolio least likely to invest directly?**

    A   Property Bond
    B   Property Unit Trust
    C   Property Company Shares
    D   Commercial Property

11. **With which of the following is the term 'forward' most commonly associated?**

    A   Equities
    B   Unit trusts
    C   Foreign exchange
    D   Insurance

12. **Which of the following is the main exchange for traded options?**

    A NYSE Liffe
    B London Stock Exchange
    C LCH.Clearnet
    D Euroclear

13. **The FTSE 100 index is comprised of**

    A Top 100 performing companies on the LSE
    B All LSE equities
    C 100 Companies selected by the Financial Times
    D Approximately the top 100 companies on LSE based on market capitalisation

14. **Which of the following is true of the Dow Jones Index?**

    A Provides a narrow view of the US equity market
    B Provides a broad view of the US equity market
    C Provides a narrow view of the US commodities market
    D Provides a broad view of the US commodities market

15. **What is the function of underwriters?**

    A To issue new shares of a company
    B To buy shares not subscribed for
    C To cancel issued shares
    D To assist companies in finding buyers for their shares

16. **What is the difference between a secured and unsecured loan?**

    A A life contract that will pay off the debt in case of default
    B A secured loan has a contractual agreement to ensure payment of the debt linked to the borrower's assets. An unsecured loan does not
    C A third party agrees to be jointly liable to the debt
    D There is no difference in risk to the lender

17. **If a company is proposing to change its constitution, what minimum percentage of eligible shareholders must vote in favour?**

    A 51%
    B 60%
    C 75%
    D 90%

18. **What is the minimum number of years that a company must have been trading to gain a full premium listing on LSE?**

    A One year
    B Two years
    C Three years
    D Five years

19. **Which of the following is a disadvantage of listing?**

    A May be subject to a takeover bid
    B Must pay a dividend to shareholders
    C Founding shareholders must sell their entire holding
    D Directors must be given free shares

20. **Which of the following is the most likely reason for gaining a listing on the Alternative Investment Market?**

    A Lower costs than borrowing
    B Gain overseas contracts
    C Takeover another company
    D Access to capital

21. **When a company issues cumulative preference shares, which of the following is the consequence?**

    A Dividends roll up to be paid on redemption
    B If a dividend cannot be paid due to lack of profits, then the dividend will still be payable at a future date when the company has sufficient funds
    C The dividend accumulates until the investor elects to take payment
    D The dividend rises each year and takes part in exceptional profits of the company

22. **Which of the following is an example of a mandatory corporate action where the investor will receive fully paid up shares?**

    A Bonus issue
    B Dividend
    C Rights issue
    D Open offer

23. **A life policy which has a sum assured of £120,000 throughout the term of the policy is known as**

    A Non-profit
    B Traditional with-profit
    C Unitised with-profit
    D Unit-linked

24. **Which of the following is not one of the FCA Principles for Businesses?**

    A Financial prudence
    B Best execution
    C Management and control
    D Clients' assets

25. **A 4% £100 nominal bond has a market price of £70. What is the current flat yield?**

    A 4%
    B 4.5%
    C 5.71%
    D 7%

26. **Which of the following is an advantage of a corporate bond?**

    A Mid-term payment
    B Ability to alter coupon frequency
    C Normally fixed term to redemption
    D Rebate for non-taxpayers on initial capital

27. **Which of the following is the best term to describe an exchange of a fixed interest payment for a floating interest payment?**

    A Forward rate agreement
    B Interest rate future
    C Interest rate swap
    D Repo

28. **You are the writer of call options in XYZ plc. What is the nature of your commitment?**

    A You are the buyer of the right to sell shares at a fixed price
    B You have bought the right to sell XYZ plc shares at a fixed price on an agreed date and you have received a premium
    C You are the buyer of the right to buy shares at a fixed price
    D You have sold the right to buy XYZ plc shares at a fixed price on an agreed date and you have received a premium

29. **Which of the following is a closed-ended fund?**

    A An investment trust, because it has a fixed number of shares
    B A unit trust, because it has a fixed capital structure
    C An investment company with variable capital, because it has a limited number of investors
    D A unit trust ISA, because it has defined tax benefits

30. **Which of the following is true of a unit trust?**

    A The Trustee is the legal owner of the trust's assets
    B The Trustee is responsible for legal and beneficial ownership of the trust's assets
    C An authorised depository is the legal owner of the assets on behalf of the Trustee
    D The unit holder is the legal owner of the trust's assets

31. **An adviser decides to raise the issue of accident insurance cover with a client. This is most probably in connection with the following financial need of the client.**

    A Buying a house with mortgage finance
    B Retirement savings
    C Estate planning
    D Tax planning

32. **Which of the following is responsible for the independent supervision of the board of an OEIC?**

    A The FCA
    B Depositary
    C Trustee
    D Treasury

33. **Which of the following is traded on the Stock Exchange?**

    A Unit trusts
    B OEICs
    C Insurance bonds
    D ETFs

34. **Which of the following is responsible for keeping the register of shareholders for an OEIC?**

    A ACD
    B Depositary
    C Trustee
    D Registrar

35. **What percentage of a Real Estate Investment Trust's profits must be distributed to shareholders in order to avoid Corporation Tax?**

    A 60%
    B 70%
    C 80%
    D 90%

36. **Which of the following is an objective of the Financial Conduct Authority under the Financial Services and Markets Act 2000, as amended?**

    A   Ensuring that the relevant markets function well
    B   Reduce the need for fraud investigations
    C   To ensure an adequate degree of protection for those working in the finance industry
    D   Promote public awareness of the London Stock Exchange

37. **If a firm's Anti-Money Laundering Officer has grounds to believe that a report should be passed on to the authorities, to which of the following should they refer the matter?**

    A   The Financial Conduct Authority
    B   Joint Money Laundering Steering Group
    C   Serious Organised Crime Agency (to become the National Crime Agency)
    D   HMRC

38. **Which of the following would constitute insider dealing?**

    A   Dealing on information believed, with reasonable grounds, to be widely available to the public
    B   Dealing to repay a debt regardless of the information held
    C   Dealing but not making a profit
    D   Dealing on unpublished information that is unavailable to the public

39. **Under the Data Protection Principles of the Data Protection Act 1998, how long may information be retained?**

    A   12 months
    B   3 years
    C   5 years
    D   As long as necessary for its purpose

40. **If a firm investigates a material complaint, what must it do when providing a final response to the complainant?**

    A   It must refer the detail of the complaint to the regulator within 48 hours
    B   It must offer the complainant an ex-gratia payment of no less than £200
    C   It must advise the complainant that they can refer the matter to the Financial Ombudsman Service if they are not happy with the firm's final response
    D   They must take independent legal advice before accepting the final response

41. An investor loses £35,000 which he placed in investments with a firm that has not been subject to regulatory authorisation and has now been wound up as insolvent. How much can the investor claim from the Financial Services Compensation Scheme?

    A Nothing
    B £17,500
    C £30,000
    D £35,000

42. Which of the following is exempt from liability to Capital Gains Tax?

    A Equities
    B Unit trust
    C Holiday home
    D Lottery prize

43. What is the earliest age that an individual may open a Cash ISA in their own name?

    A From birth
    B 14
    C 16
    D 18

44. At what age will the child be able to make withdrawals from a Junior ISA?

    A 12
    B 14
    C 16
    D 18

45. Which of the following is also known a Defined Benefit Scheme?

    A Money purchase
    B Final salary
    C Protected rights
    D Retirement annuity

46. Which of the following is not subject to Capital Gains Tax on its disposal?

    A Eurobond
    B Unit trust
    C OEIC
    D Gilt

47. **A gift is exempt from inheritance tax if it is made to the donor's**

    A   Child
    B   Civil partner
    C   Parent
    D   Sibling

48. **Who is the legal owner of a trust's assets?**

    A   Settlor
    B   Trustee
    C   Creator
    D   Beneficiary

49. **A lender X quotes an interest rate on a loan of 12%. Interest will be charged monthly. What is the effective annual rate?**

    A   12.0%
    B   12.68%
    C   12.84%
    D   11.4%

50. **What is the main reason why the UK mortgage market is larger than in most other EU countries?**

    A   More people in the UK tend to own their own home
    B   Renting is not as popular in the EU as in the UK
    C   Mortgages are controlled in some EU states
    D   In some EU countries, each mortgage must be individually approved by Government

Answers

1. **D**   Personal investors are the main clients in the retail sector
   BPP Study Text Chapter 1 Section 8.1 / CISI Workbook Chapter 1 Section 2

2. **D**   A custodian is responsible for looking after the assets of fund managers and so on
   BPP Study Text Chapter 1 Section 3.9 / CISI Workbook Chapter 1 Section 4.9

3. **D**   The Bank of England's Monetary Policy Committee sets short-term interest rates in the UK
   BPP Study Text Chapter 1 Section 2.2.4 / CISI Workbook Chapter 2 Section 3.2.1

4. **B**   Bank lending leads to credit creation
   BPP Study Text Chapter 1 Section 1.7 / CISI Workbook Chapter 2 Section 4.1

5. **B**   Borrowers are likely to benefit most from inflation
   BPP Study Text Chapter 1 Section 1.8.3 / CISI Workbook Chapter 2 Section 4.2

6. **D**   Interest is paid gross without deduction of tax
   BPP Study Text Chapter 7 Section 1.4 / CISI Workbook Chapter 3 Section 2

7. **C**   £3,000 x 4.5% = £135 and £17,000 x 4.5% = £765

   £765 x 80% = £612 (after tax is deducted at source)

   Monetary amount received at the end of the year = £135 + £612 = £747

   There will be a further tax liability of £153 to pay at a later point as the investor is a 40% taxpayer
   BPP Study Text Chapter 4 Section 1 and Chapter 7 Section 7.1 / CISI Workbook Chapter 3 Section 2

8. **B**   Treasury Bill auctions are held weekly
   BPP Study Text Chapter 2 Section 10.2 / CISI Workbook Chapter 3 Section 3

9. **C**   Coupon is the name for interest on a bond
   BPP Study Text Chapter 2 Section 8.2.4 / CISI Workbook Chapter 5 Section 2

10. **D**   Commercial property is the least likely investment
    BPP Study Text Chapter 4 Section 2.1 / CISI Workbook Chapter 3 Section 4

11. **C**   Forward rates are commonly associated with the currency market
    BPP Study Text Chapter 1 Section 7.3 / CISI Workbook Chapter 3 Section 5

12. **A**   NYSE Liffe is the main exchange for traded options
    BPP Study Text Chapter 1 Section 6.2 / CISI Workbook Chapter 6 Section 5.2.1

Introduction to Securities and Investment ♦ Practice Examination 1 – Answers

13. **D** Market capitalisation determines entry to and exit from the FTSE 100
    BPP Study Text Chapter 2 Section 5.2 / CISI Workbook Chapter 4 Section 9.1

14. **A** The DJIA represents 30 US industrial shares, selected by committee, and therefore provides only a narrow view on the US equity market
    BPP Study Text Chapter 2 Section 5.2 / CISI Workbook Chapter 4 Section 9

15. **B** Underwriters provide a guarantee for the issuing companies against unsold shares
    BPP Study Text Chapter 2 Section 3.4.3 / CISI Workbook Chapter 4 Section 6.2

16. **B** There is a contract linking payment of the debt to the borrower's assets
    BPP Study Text Chapter 4 Section 5.3 / CISI Workbook Chapter 10 Section 1.3

17. **C** A Special Resolution is required. 75% of those voting must vote in favour
    BPP Study Text Chapter 2 Section 1.4 / CISI Workbook Chapter 4 Section 2.3

18. **C** A three year track record is required to gain a premium listing
    BPP Study Text Chapter 2 Section 4.3 / CISI Workbook Chapter 4 Section 7.2.1

19. **A** Listed companies may be subject to a takeover bid
    BPP Study Text Chapter 2 Section 4.2 / CISI Workbook Chapter 4 Section 7.2

20. **D** The major benefit of becoming AIM-quoted is access to new capital
    BPP Study Text Chapter 2 Section 4.3 / CISI Workbook Chapter 4 Section 7.2.2

21. **B** 'Cumulative' implies that, if the dividend is unpaid, it will accumulate to be paid in a subsequent year
    BPP Study Text Chapter 2 Section 2.2 / CISI Workbook Chapter 4 Section 3.2

22. **A** Bonus issues are mandatory and lead to fully paid up shares being issued
    BPP Study Text Chapter 2 Section 3.2 / CISI Workbook Chapter 4 Section 6

23. **A** A sum assured which remains unchanged is characteristic of a non-profit policy
    BPP Study Text Chapter 4 Section 7 / CISI Workbook Chapter 10 Section 3.1

24. **B** This is a conduct of business rule rather than one of the Principles for Businesses
    BPP Study Text Chapter 6 Sections 1.5 / CISI Workbook Chapter 8 Section 1.3

25. **C** $4/70 \times 100 = 5.71\%$. Flat yield is coupon/price $\times$ 100
    BPP Study Text Chapter 2 Section 9.7 / CISI Workbook Chapter 5 Section 5.2

26. **C** Corporate bonds normally have a fixed term to redemption
    BPP Study Text Chapter 2 Section 9.1 / CISI Workbook Chapter 5 Section 2

Introduction to Securities and Investment ♦ Practice Examination 1 – Answers

27. **C** A swap is an exchange of different types of interest payment for an agreed amount at an agreed price

BPP Study Text Chapter 3 Section 5 / CISI Workbook Chapter 6 Section 4.2

28. **D** You are the writer, so you sold the option to someone else. As it is a call option, it gives them the right to buy shares from you at an agreed price. You were paid a premium to undertake this obligation

BPP Study Text Chapter 3 Section 3.3.2 / CISI Workbook Chapter 6 Section 3

29. **A** An investment trust is a closed ended fund. Companies generally, except the special case of OEICs, are closed-ended

BPP Study Text Chapter 5 Section 4.1 / CISI Workbook Chapter 7 Section 5

30. **A** The trustee of a unit trust is the legal owner of the trust's assets. The beneficial owners are the unitholders

BPP Study Text Chapter 5 Section 2.1 / CISI Workbook Chapter 7 Section 2

31. **A** Accident insurance can help cover a homebuyer's mortgage commitments following an accident

BPP Study Text Chapter 4 Section 7 / CISI Workbook Chapter 10 Section 3.3

32. **B** The Depositary supervises the ACD. The FCA is the regulator of OEICs

BPP Study Text Chapter 5 Section 3.2 / CISI Workbook Chapter 7 Section 3

33. **D** ETFs are exchange traded funds and, as their name implies, trade on the Stock Exchange

BPP Study Text Chapter 5 Section 5 / CISI Workbook Chapter 7 Section 7

34. **A** The ACD (authorised corporate director) is the registrar for an OEIC

BPP Study Text Chapter 5 Section 3.3 / CISI Workbook Chapter 7 Section 3

35. **D** 90% of profits need to be paid to investors, to benefit from the corporation tax exemption

BPP Study Text Chapter 5 Section 7 / CISI Workbook Chapter 7 Section 6

36. **A** 'Ensuring that the relevant markets function well' is the FCA's single strategic objective

BPP Study Text Chapter 6 Section 1.2.2 / CISI Workbook Chapter 8 Section 1.2.1

37. **C** Referrals would be made to the SOCA (to become the NCA)

BPP Study Text Chapter 6 Section 2.5.1 / CISI Workbook Chapter 8 Section 2.1.3

38. **D** Dealing on information that is not available to the public. The others are defences against insider dealing

BPP Study Text Chapter 6 Section 3.2 / CISI Workbook Chapter 8 Section 3

39. **D** Information may only be retained for as long as is necessary for its purpose

BPP Study Text Chapter 6 Section 4 / CISI Workbook Chapter 8 Section 5

40.	C	Reference to the FOS must be made in the final response to the complainant
		BPP Study Text Chapter 6 Section 5.1.1 / CISI Workbook Chapter 8 Section 6.1
41.	A	Given that the firm was not authorised, there is no compensation payment
		BPP Study Text Chapter 6 Section 5.3 / CISI Workbook Chapter 8 Section 6.4
42.	D	Betting, lottery and pools winnings are exempt from CGT
		BPP Study Text Chapter 7 Section 2.2 / CISI Workbook Chapter 9 Section 2.2
43.	C	16 years is the earliest age that it is possible to open a cash ISA in the person's own name. A Junior cash ISA may be opened for someone who is under 16, by a person with parental responsibility, but not by the child before age 16
		BPP Study Text Chapter 7 Section 7 / CISI Workbook Chapter 9 Section 3.1
44.	D	Withdrawals are not permitted until after the child's 18th birthday
		BPP Study Text Chapter 7 Section 7.4 / CISI Workbook Chapter 9 Section 3.2
45.	B	Final salary schemes are also known as Defined Benefit Schemes
		BPP Study Text Chapter 4 Section 3.3 / CISI Workbook Chapter 9 Section 4.4
46.	D	Gilts are exempt from CGT
		BPP Study Text Chapter 7 Section 2.2 / CISI Workbook Chapter 9 Section 2.2
47.	B	The tax rules for same-sex civil partners are the same as for spouses. Gifts to spouses and civil partners are exempt from IHT
		BPP Study Text Chapter 7 Section 3.3 / CISI Workbook Chapter 9 Section 2.3
48.	B	The trustee is the legal owner of the assets from a trust
		BPP Study Text Chapter 7 Section 8.2 / CISI Workbook Chapter 9 Section 6
49.	B	1% monthly. $1.01^{12} = 1.1268$, so 12.68%
		BPP Study Text Chapter 4 Section 5.2 / CISI Workbook Chapter 10 Section 1.4
50.	A	UK residents typically prefer to buy rather than rent
		BPP Study Text Chapter 4 Section 6 / CISI Workbook Chapter 10 Section 2.1

Practice Examination 2

50 Questions in 1 Hour

1. Which of the following is most closely associated with forward transactions?

   A Insurance transaction
   B Foreign exchange transaction
   C Equity transaction
   D Unit trust transaction

2. Which of the following is true of preference shares?

   A They always receive a dividend even if there are no profits
   B The dividend is never cumulative
   C A dividend level is fixed as a percentage of their nominal value on issue
   D Holders receive interest but the dividend is retained for the benefit of the company

3. Which of the following is likely to benefit most from high inflation?

   A Saver
   B Earner of a fixed income
   C Borrower
   D Exporters

4. Which of the following describes the creation of credit?

   A Bank lending more than it has in its reserves
   B Businesses paying creditors promptly
   C Paying by cash rather than cheque
   D Treasury printing more notes and coins

5. Which of the following is the purpose of the Monetary Policy Committee?

   A To control inflation through the use of interest rates
   B Recommend an inflation target to the Treasury
   C Set the current rate of inflation
   D To measure the current level of money supply

6. Which of the following is a function of the Bank of England?

- A Acts as the Government's banker
- B Regulates building societies
- C Recommends an inflation target to the Treasury
- D Approves the authorisation of financial services firms

7. A corporate action is an event affecting

- A The truth and fairness of the financial statements
- B The articles of association
- C The group structure
- D Either bondholders or shareholders

8. On which exchange do the 'soft commodities' trade?

- A NYSE Liffe
- B London Stock Exchange
- C London Metal Exchange
- D ICE Futures

9. Which of the following is true for a private limited company?

- A If it wishes to issue shares to the public, the issue must have approval from Companies House
- B 75% of shareholders must vote in favour of issuing shares to the public
- C It is not possible to issue shares to the public
- D It is possible to issue shares to the public but a maximum block of only 1,000 shares per person can be issued

10. A firm's anti-money laundering regulations typically require a new individual client to provide identity showing the person's name, and what else?

- A Age
- B Address
- C Date of birth
- D Place of birth

11. Which of the following carry full voting entitlement?

- A Preference shares
- B Debentures
- C A Class shares
- D Ordinary shares

12. Which of the following is true following a capitalisation issue?

    A The number of shares held will change
    B The price per shares will remain the same
    C There will be a repayment to the shareholder of capital
    D The shareholder will have to sell some of his/her holding

13. How would a certificated holding be settled?

    A Through Book Entry Transfer
    B Through providing a share certificate and signed transfer form
    C By notifying the registrar
    D By filling in the form of renunciation on the back of the certificate

14. Which of the following is an advantage of a company gaining a listing?

    A It will be more accountable to its shareholders
    B It must meet the LSE information requirements
    C It has greater access to capital
    D It has more control over how it spends it capital

15. A bond has a coupon of 7% maturing in 2015. Its current price is 112. What is the bond's flat yield?

    A 7.0%
    B 6.25%
    C 7.95%
    D 12.0%

16. A firm receives a complaint. What is the maximum time the firm has to send a holding or final response?

    A Five days
    B Ten days
    C Four weeks
    D Eight weeks

17. Which of the following is the best definition of a gilt?

    A Short-term debt issued at a discount to par
    B Debt instrument issued by a company with a fixed coupon
    C Debt instrument issued by the Government to fund spending in excess of receipts
    D Debt instrument issued by local government to fund spending in excess of statutory funding

18. A large company has decided to undertake a review of its responsibilities to its stakeholders. Suggestions for whom the review could cover include employees, shareholders, suppliers and customers. Which of these might it reasonably conclude are among its stakeholders?

    A Employees and shareholders only
    B Shareholders and customers only
    C Shareholders, suppliers and customers only
    D Employees, shareholders, suppliers and customers

19. How are gilts issued?

    A By auction through the DMO
    B By auction conducted on LSE
    C By fixed offer through the LSE
    D By placing through the LSE

20. A short-dated gilt is a gilt with a life of less than

    A One year
    B Three years
    C Seven years
    D Ten years

21. An agreement to deliver a standard quantity of a specified asset at a future date at a price agreed today is a

    A Put
    B Call
    C Forward
    D Future

22. Classifications for UK funds (unit trusts and OEICs) are published by

    A The Investment Management Association
    B The UK Listing Authority
    C The Association of Investment Companies
    D The Financial Conduct Authority

23. For a retail bank account, it is possible to determine the net rate for basic rate taxpayers from the gross equivalent amount by

    A Deducting 10% savings tax from the gross amount
    B Deducting 20% income tax from the gross amount
    C An R85 adjustment
    D A P11D adjustment

24. Norman wishes his dependants to receive a lump sum when he dies. Which of the following investments would be the most suitable?

   A A five year term assurance policy
   B Critical illness cover
   C A whole of life policy
   D Capital protected guaranteed bond

25. Which of the following is the essential feature of a mortgage?

   A An unsecured loan to purchase property
   B An equitable charge to the borrower
   C Assigns the repayment vehicle to the lender
   D Provides security for a loan in the form of property

26. A five-year capped mortgage where the borrower pays no more than a maximum amount can be described as

   A Discounted rate
   B Variable rate
   C Five-year fixed rate
   D Base rate tracker

27. Which is a characteristic of a non-profit whole of life policy?

   A A fixed sum assured
   B Exempt from inheritance tax on payment
   C A return linked to stock market performance
   D Would accept an additional life assured

28. Under a stakeholder pension plan opened in the current year, what is the maximum charge that can be made for transfers into or out of the fund?

   A 1% of fund value at time of transfer
   B No transfer charges are allowed
   C £20 net
   D £20 gross

29. Which of the following describes a pension scheme that will provide an income linked to earnings at or close to the retirement age?

   A Contracted out money purchase scheme
   B Executive pension plan
   C Final salary scheme
   D Deferred income scheme

30. What are the maximum annual charges that can be imposed on a stakeholder pension plan opened in the current tax year?

   A £100
   B 1.5% of the fund value
   C £1 per month
   D 1% of the bid/offer price

31. What is the minimum amount of net taxable profits that a REIT must distribute if it is to remain exempt from corporation tax?

   A 70%
   B 80%
   C 90%
   D 100%

32. Which of the following best describes the function of the Depositary in relation to an OEIC?

   A Is responsible for the management of the OEIC and retaining the register
   B Is the point of contact for the sale and redemption of Shares
   C Has custody of the assets and oversees the ACD to ensure that it complies with the Instrument of Incorporation and prospectus
   D Is responsible for establishing a board of directors to run the OEIC

33. The Articles of Association do not require the private company Court Wellington Ltd to hold an Annual General Meeting each year but the company is required to hold an AGM this year. This is because

   A The company will consider a resolution to dismiss a director
   B Fifteen months will have elapsed since the last time an AGM was held
   C Members holding over 1% of voting shares have demanded that an AGM be held
   D The Companies Act 2006 requires all companies to hold an AGM

34. What would be the correct term for the type of advice that can be defined as follows? 'A personal recommendation to a retail client in relation to a retail investment product which is not independent advice, or alternatively is basic advice on stakeholder products, using pre-scripted questions.'

   A Designated investment advice
   B Limited advice
   C Restricted advice
   D Depolarised advice

35. The term 'closed-ended' applied to an investment trust indicates that it

- A Is not available to new retail investors
- B Has a fixed lifespan
- C Has a limited number of shares in issue
- D Cannot be advertised

36. Which of the following will be decided by a vote at the company's annual general meeting?

- A Appointment of divisional managers
- B Appointment of directors
- C Purchase of fixed assets
- D Operational strategy decisions

37. What does 'UCITS' stand for?

- A Unified Consolidated Investment Trading Service
- B Underwritten Corporate Issues Trading System
- C Undertakings for Collective Investments in Transferable Securities
- D Unlimited Companies for Investments in Traded Swaps

38. Which of the following does not accurately describe one of the FCA's statutory objectives?

- A Ensuring that the relevant markets function well
- B Protecting and enhancing the integrity of the UK financial system
- C Secure the appropriate degree of protection for consumers
- D Detecting and reducing threats to the financial system as a whole

39. Who would normally report a suspicious transaction to the Serious Organised Crime Agency (to become the National Crime Agency)?

- A The employee
- B The Money Laundering Reporting Officer of the firm
- C The Chief Executive of the firm
- D The Joint Money Laundering Steering Group, after consulting with the firm's Compliance Department

40. The interest received on a bond is its

- A Yield
- B Coupon
- C Dividend
- D Debenture

41. A firm which has completed dealing with a material complaint must, as part of the final response:

    A   Offer an ex-gratia payment of at least £20 as a gesture of goodwill
    B   Send a copy of the complaints procedure
    C   Inform the complainant of their right to refer to Financial Ombudsman Service
    D   Inform the regulator within three working days of the detail of the complaint

42. Who can pay money in to the Junior ISA of a child before the child reaches age 16?

    A   Any person
    B   Members of the immediate family and grandparents of the child only
    C   Members of the immediate family of the child only
    D   The registered contact for the account only

43. Which independent body regulates how an OEIC operates?

    A   Financial Conduct Authority
    B   Depository
    C   Authorised Corporate Director
    D   Her Majesty's Treasury

44. With regard to life assurance, which of the following is true?

    A   Term assurance will normally have a surrender value
    B   Whole of life policies will only pay out if death occurs within a specified term
    C   With-profits policies guarantee a sum upon death plus a possible terminal bonus
    D   Unit-linked policies create a certain sum of money payable if death occurs within a specified term

45. Under which of the following circumstances would a claim be made on the Financial Services Compensation Scheme?

    A   Where the firm involved is declared insolvent
    B   Where an approved person working for the firm acted in a negligent manner
    C   Where an approved person working for the firm acted in a fraudulent manner
    D   Where the regulator has withdrawn its permission for the firm to conduct investment business

46. Which of the following is an index for the stock market of Germany?

    A   CAC
    B   DAX
    C   Mibtel
    D   Nikkei 225

47. **You borrow some money from the bank and are quoted a rate of 8% payable quarterly. What is the effective annual rate you will pay?**

    A 8.0%

    B 7.76%

    C 8.24%

    D 2.0%

48. **Which of the following best describes the function of a market maker?**

    A To forecast the prices at which they will transact

    B Quote the size and price at which they will transact

    C They are not for profit organisations designed to create an orderly market

    D They will report trades via the SETS system

49. **A lending banking is quoting a simple rate of interest on a loan, with no charges. The effective annual rate on the loan will be the same unless**

    A Interest is paid in advance instead of in arrears

    B Interest is paid more often than once per year

    C The loan is secured

    D The loan is to a charity

50. **What compensation would you expect if you lost £45,000 in protected investments with a firm that had become insolvent?**

    A £50,000

    B £40,500

    C £45,000

    D £22,500

Answers

1. **B** Forward transactions are commonly associated with the forex (FX) market where a deal is conducted at an agreed price and date in the future. This compares to a future which is an agreement to buy or sell a standard amount of a specified asset on a fixed date at a fixed price. Futures are tradable whereas forwards are not

   BPP Study Text Chapter 1 Section 7.3 / CISI Workbook Chapter 3 Section 5

2. **C** The dividend on preference shares is a fixed dividend expressed as a percentage of nominal value. Preference shares are usually (but not always) cumulative. While the preference dividend must be paid before an ordinary dividend is paid and may be paid in years where the company has made no profits, preference shareholders have no automatic right to the dividend, which is paid at the discretion of the company

   BPP Study Text Chapter 2 Section 2.2 / CISI Workbook Chapter 4 Section 3.2

3. **C** A saver will be earning a set amount of interest on his savings and high inflation will mean that his money can buy less and less as time goes by. This is even more the case for an earner or receiver of a fixed income such as a pensioner. In addition an exporter will sell his goods at a fixed price and this will also be eroded with high inflation. However a borrower is most likely to benefit since the amount owing will lose value in comparison to earnings (which tend to increase faster than inflation)

   BPP Study Text Chapter 1 Section 1.8.3 / CISI Workbook Chapter 2 Section 4.2

4. **A** Banks lending more than reserves is the main method of credit creation. When a business pays its creditors promptly, it is simply paying what was is due into the system – which is not 'new' money. Paying in cash compared to a cheque is also not 'new' money. Although printing more notes and coins can contribute to creating credit, it is usually accompanied by the withdrawal of old notes and coins

   BPP Study Text Chapter 1 Section 1.7 / CISI Workbook Chapter 2 Section 4.1

5. **A** The inflation target is set each year by The Chancellor to the Exchequer, not by the Bank. Nobody sets a rate of inflation – it is something which is measured. The Bank may well measure money supply but the question specifically relates to the Monetary Policy Committee whose function is indeed to control inflation through interest rates

   BPP Study Text Chapter 1 Section 2.2.4 / CISI Workbook Chapter 2 Section 3.2.1

6. **A** The Bank of England does not recommend an inflation target to the Treasury. (The Treasury has enough of its own economists who can do that!) The BoE, as a central bank, is indeed the Government's banker

   BPP Study Text Chapter 1 Section 2.2 / CISI Workbook Chapter 2 Section 3.2

7. **D** A corporate action is an event affecting bondholders or shareholders, such as a dividend or coupon payment

   BPP Study Text Chapter 2 Section 3 / CISI Workbook Chapter 4 Section 6

8. **A** The London Stock Exchange is a market for securities. As its name suggests, the London Metal Exchange trades base metal derivatives, and ICE Futures is concerned with energy derivatives. Soft commodities, such as sugar, wheat and cocoa, are traded on NYSE Liffe

BPP Study Text Chapter 1 Section 5.1 / CISI Workbook Chapter 6 Section 5.2.1

9. **C** It is not possible for a private limited company to issue shares to the public. Therefore all the other answers are 'red herrings'

BPP Study Text Chapter 2 Section 1.1 / CISI Workbook Chapter 4 Section 7.2.1

10. **B** It is necessary to establish satisfactory evidence of identity. The name and address is typically a minimum requirement. How much identity information to ask for, and what to verify, are matters for the judgement of the firm, based on its assessment of risk

BPP Study Text Chapter 6 Section 2.8 / CISI Workbook Chapter 8 Section 2.1.3

11. **D** Debentures are a form of debt set against fixed charges and, as such, have no voting rights. Normally, preference shares have no voting rights but could acquire voting rights in circumstances where their dividend had not been paid for five years. Class A shares are shares in the company but specifically exclude voting rights. It is the ordinary shares of a company that carry full voting rights

BPP Study Text Chapter 2 Section 2.1 / CISI Workbook Chapter 4 Section 3

12. **A** The number of shares will change as there will be more after the bonus issue but their price will fall proportionately to the increase in shares. Reserves are used to create the new shares but no money actually changes hands. There is no requirement for the shareholder to sell (nor buy) any of his holding

BPP Study Text Chapter 2 Section 3.2 / CISI Workbook Chapter 4 Section 6

13. **B** The certificate and signed transfer form must be provided. The other answers are incorrect

BPP Study Text Chapter 2 Section 2.8 / CISI Workbook Chapter 4 Section 11

14. **C** Neither being more accountable to shareholders nor being subject to information requirements from the LSE can be seen as an advantage. In addition, by listing itself, a company is likely to have less, and not more, control of how it spends its capital. However a listed company has greater access to capital than a non-listed company and hence this is an advantage

BPP Study Text Chapter 2 Section 4.1 / CISI Workbook Chapter 4 Section 7.2

15. **B** Flat yield is calculated as (coupon divided by price) × 100. In this case it would be (7 / 112) × 100 = 6.25%

BPP Study Text Chapter 2 Section 9.7 / CISI Workbook Chapter 5 Section 5.2

16. **D** A firm has to send a holding or final response within eight weeks

BPP Study Text Chapter 6 Section 5.1.1 / CISI Workbook Chapter 8 Section 6.1

17. **C** Firstly, gilts can be short-term as well as long-term (for example, there has been the issue of a 50-year gilt in recent years). Secondly, gilts are issued by the government and not by companies nor by local authorities. They are debt instrument issued to finance the PSNCR

BPP Study Text Chapter 2 Section 8.1 / CISI Workbook Chapter 5 Section 3

| 18. | D | Large companies are increasingly being held to account for their interactions with all groups whom their activities touch |

BPP Study Text Chapter 6 Section 7.10 / CISI Workbook Chapter 8 Section 7.3

| 19. | A | The primary market is through the auction by the DMO. The LSE is involved in trading Gilts once they have been issued but is not involved in their original issuance |

BPP Study Text Chapter 2 Section 8.3 / CISI Workbook Chapter 5 Section 3.3

| 20. | C | By DMO definitions, a gilt with less than seven years to run is 'short-dated' |

BPP Study Text Chapter 2 Section 8.4 / CISI Workbook Chapter 5 Section 3.2

| 21. | D | A Put is the right but not an obligation to sell an asset and a Call is the right but not the obligation to buy an asset. A Forward is a derivative trade done over the counter (OTC): as such, it enables the parties to the trade to tailor the trade to their actual needs. A Future is an agreement to buy or sell a standard quantity of a specified asset on a fixed future date at a price agreed today. That is, a future does not have the flexibility of a forward |

BPP Study Text Chapter 1 Section 7.3 and Chapter 3 Sections 2.1 and 3 / CISI Workbook Chapter 6 Section 2

| 22. | A | As the trade body for UK open-ended funds, the IMA produces these classifications |

BPP Study Text Chapter 5 Section 1.3 / CISI Workbook Chapter 7 Section 1.4

| 23. | B | The net amount is the gross less 20% tax on interest. The bank will normally withhold the 20% at source, although non-taxpayers can elect to receive interest gross by completing the HMRC form R85. The P11D has nothing to do with interest earned: it concerns benefits-in-kind provided by an employer, such as medical insurance |

BPP Study Text Chapter 4 Section 1 / CISI Workbook Chapter 3 Section 2

| 24. | C | The whole of life policy will be the most appropriate as it will pay a lump sum when Norman dies and not just within a specific term |

BPP Study Text Chapter 4 Section 7 / CISI Workbook Chapter 10 Section 3

| 25. | D | One might be tempted to select option A – a loan to purchase a property. While a mortgage is generally a loan to purchase a property, this is a specific use of a mortgage. The best definition of a mortgage however is a secured loan, because a mortgage could be used for things other than property |

BPP Study Text Chapter 4 Section 6 / CISI Workbook Chapter 10 Section 2.2

| 26. | C | A capped mortgage does not have to have a life of five years, of course |

BPP Study Text Chapter 4 Section 6.4 / CISI Workbook Chapter 10 Section 2.4

| 27. | A | A whole of life policy will pay out on the death of the life insured and such payments would be included in their estate for IHT purposes. A non-profit whole of life policy has no link to stock market performance and the acceptance or not of an additional life assured is irrelevant. As stated, it is a policy for a fixed sum assured |

BPP Study Text Chapter 4 Section 7 / CISI Workbook Chapter 10 Section 3.1

Introduction to Securities and Investment ♦ Practice Examination 2 – Answers

28. **B**   No charges are allowed in relation to a stakeholder pension transfer

   BPP Study Text Chapter 4 Section 3.6 / CISI Workbook Chapter 9 Section 4.6

29. **C**   Final salary schemes are a form of occupational pension scheme where the employer guarantees to pay a fraction of pre-retirement pay to the retired individual. These are also known as defined benefit schemes

   BPP Study Text Chapter 4 Section 3.3 / CISI Workbook Chapter 9 Section 4.4

30. **B**   For new plans, charges are limited to 1.5% of the fund value for the first 10 years and then 1% thereafter. Since you did not have an option showing '1%', there should have been no confusion and 1.5% is the best answer

   BPP Study Text Chapter 4 Section 3.6 / CISI Workbook Chapter 9 Section 4.6

31. **C**   A REIT must distribute at least 90% of its taxable profits if it is to remain exempt from corporation tax

   BPP Study Text Chapter 5 Section 7 / CISI Workbook Chapter 7 Section 6

32. **C**   A Depositary in an OEIC is the equivalent of a Trustee in a Unit Trust in that he/she has custody of the assets and serves in an oversight function overseeing the activities of the Authorised Corporate Director who manages the OEIC

   BPP Study Text Chapter 5 Section 3.2 / CISI Workbook Chapter 7 Section 3

33. **A**   The removal by CA 2006 of the requirement for private companies to hold an AGM enables private companies to make many decisions by written resolution, although the company will still need to hold meetings to dismiss a director or to remove an auditor before the end of his term of office. Members holding 10% of the paid-up share capital (or 5% in certain limited circumstances for private companies) may demand that a meeting is held

   BPP Study Text Chapter 2 Section 1.4 / CISI Workbook Chapter 4 Section 2.3

34. **C**   Advice to retail customers may be restricted advice or it may be independent advice

   BPP Study Text Chapter 1 Section 9.1 / CISI Workbook Chapter 1 Section 5.1

35. **C**   As a company trading on the Stock Exchange, an investment trust is set up like any other public company with a certain amount of authorised and issued capital and shares. 'Closed-ended' refers to a limited number of shares in issue. It is known as 'closed end' since its authorised and issued capital can only be altered via changes to its memorandum of Association. An 'open ended' fund can vary its capital at will

   BPP Study Text Chapter 5 Section 4.1 / CISI Workbook Chapter 7 Section 5

36. **B**   The AGM will cover appointment of directors. The other decisions are matters for the Board or senior management

   BPP Study Text Chapter 2 Section 1.4.2 / CISI Workbook Chapter 4 Section 2.3

37. **C**   'UCITS' stands for Undertakings for Collective Investments in Transferable Securities

   BPP Study Text Chapter 5 Section 2.9 / CISI Workbook Chapter 7 Section 1.5.2

38.	**D**	Options A, B and C are statutory objectives under FSMA 2000. Option A is the strategic objective of the Authority, while B and C are operational objectives. The fourth objective – concerning the financial system as a whole – is part of the task of the Bank of England

BPP Study Text Chapter 6 Section 1.2.2 / CISI Workbook Chapter 8 Section 1.2.1

39.	**B**	The firm should make clear that an employee with suspicions should pass such suspicions on to the MLRO. The MLRO is the conduit through which a firm reports suspicious transactions to SOCA/NCA

BPP Study Text Chapter 6 Sections 2.5 / CISI Workbook Chapter 8 Section 2.1.3

40.	**B**	Interest received on a bond is the coupon. Dividends are paid on shares. A debenture is a type of corporate bond. The yield is a measure of relative return

BPP Study Text Chapter 2 Section 8.1 / CISI Workbook Chapter 5 Section 2

41.	**C**	If an authorised firm receives a complaint and it does not get resolved within 24 hours then, as part of its final response, which must be made no later than eight weeks from the complaint being received, it must advise the client of his/her right to refer his/her complaint to the Financial Ombudsman Service (FOS). The client then has a maximum of six months to do so for the complaint to receive attention from FOS

BPP Study Text Chapter 6 Section 5.1 / CISI Workbook Chapter 8 Section 6.1

42.	**D**	Any person can pay money in to a valid JISA

BPP Study Text Chapter 7 Section 7.4 / CISI Workbook Chapter 9 Section 3.2

43.	**A**	Since an OEIC is involved in carrying out regulated activities, such as dealing in shares, it must be authorised and its conduct regulated by the FCA in accordance with s19 of FSMA 2000

BPP Study Text Chapter 5 Section 3.3 / CISI Workbook Chapter 7 Section 1.5.1

44.	**C**	Term assurance normally has no surrender or maturity value. Whole of life policies will pay out regardless of when death occurs. Unit-linked policies have a direct link with the performance of the underlying fund, the value of which may fluctuate

BPP Study Text Chapter 4 Section 7 / CISI Workbook Chapter 10 Section 3.1

45.	**A**	B, C and D would certainly attract the attention of the regulator and may result in fines being imposed against a firm. However, a claim can only be made under the FSCS when a firm fails

BPP Study Text Chapter 6 Section 5.3 / CISI Workbook Chapter 8 Section 6.4

46.	**B**	The CAC index relates to France (Paris); The Nikkei relates to Japan (Tokyo) and the Mibtel relates to Italy (Milan). The index for the stock market of Germany is indeed the Dax

BPP Study Text Chapter 2 Section 6.2 / CISI Workbook Chapter 4 Section 9.1

47.	**C**	If the rate is 8% payable quarterly, then you will pay 2% each quarter. To calculate the Effective Annual Rate, you need to take 1.02 to the power 4, subtract 1, and multiply the result by 100. This comes to (1.0824 – 1) x 100 = 0.0824 x 100 = 8.24

BPP Study Text Chapter 4 Section 5.2 / CISI Workbook Chapter 10 Section 1.4

Introduction to Securities and Investment ♦ Practice Examination 2 – Answers

48. **B** Answers C and D are unrelated to the activities of market makers. Answer A is also incorrect because market makers are not forecasting prices but quoting prices and sizes of transactions at which they will deal

    BPP Study Text Chapter 2 Section 6.4 / CISI Workbook Chapter 4 Section 10

49. **B** Answers C and D are 'red herrings' and are incorrect. Answer A can have an effect on equivalent rates but this question refers to a simple interest quotation for a loan and it is convention that, unless otherwise stated, it would be on an annual basis. The effective rate of interest on the loan will be the same as the simple rate providing that the interest is only paid once per year. If interest is paid more often, then the effective rate will be higher. This is why the correct answer is B

    BPP Study Text Chapter 4 Sections 5.1 and 5.2 / CISI Workbook Chapter 10 Section 1.4

50. **C** The amount is calculated as 100% of the first £50,000

    BPP Study Text Chapter 6 Section 5.3 / CISI Workbook Chapter 8 Section 6.4

Practice Examination 3

50 Questions in 1 Hour

1. Which of the following has the primary purpose of raising finance for businesses?

    A   Hedge fund
    B   Securities house
    C   Investment bank
    D   Bank of England

2. The standard settlement timeframe for a currency transaction is

    A   T + 1
    B   T + 2
    C   T + 3
    D   T + 5

3. An investor owns £8,000 of Treasury 8% 2021 when it is trading at a market price of £106. What is the flat yield?

    A   7.5%
    B   6.0%
    C   8.0%
    D   6.5%

4. What is normally the effect of credit creation?

    A   Increase in money supply
    B   Increase in balance of payments deficit
    C   Decrease in inflation
    D   Increase in unemployment

5. Which is the measure used to determine the level of imports and exports?

    A   Retail Prices Index
    B   Base rate
    C   Public Sector Net Cash Requirement
    D   Balance of payments

6. Which of the following is not a part of the Bank of England?

   A Financial Policy Committee
   B Financial Conduct Authority
   C Prudential Regulation Authority
   D Monetary Policy Committee

7. What might be the main advantage of someone who already has income protection insurance (IPI) cover taking out critical illness insurance cover in addition?

   A To pay periodic benefits above the amounts provided by IPI
   B To provide cover in the event of an accident
   C To pay benefits after retirement age
   D To provide a lump sum payment

8. What would be the most likely effect of an increase in the PSNCR?

   A Higher unemployment
   B Reduction in balance of payments deficit
   C Reduction in GDP
   D An increase in inflation

9. Which of the following is a reason to invest in a fixed term deposit rather than an 'instant access' account?

   A Benefit from a higher level of protection from the Financial Services Compensation Scheme
   B Maximisation of tax benefits
   C Benefit from a higher rate of interest
   D Lower risk of default

10. Which type of market are money market instruments generally considered to service?

    A Short-term wholesale cash market
    B Long-term wholesale cash market
    C Short-term retail cash market
    D Long-term retail cash market

11. In which of the following types of property is an institutional investor least likely to invest?

    A Residential property
    B Small commercial property
    C Industrial property
    D Farmland property

12. Which of the following is an index for the stock market of France?

    A CAC 40
    B Mibtel
    C Nikkei 225
    D Dax

13. Which of the following is a restriction placed on private limited companies?

    A Any sale of the company must be approved by Companies House
    B Shares may not be sold in blocks of more than 1000 shares
    C Shares may not be issued to the public
    D Any sale of the company must be approved by 75% of shareholders

14. Who can pay money into a Junior ISA that is in the name of a child aged under 16?

    A The child who holds the account or a person with parental responsibility only
    B A person with parental responsibility only
    C A person with parental responsibility or a grandparent only
    D Anyone

15. The Alternative Investment Market exists mainly to allow investment in

    A Large multinational companies
    B Smaller, growing companies
    C UK large companies
    D Derivatives

16. Where stock is held in electronic accounts, this is referred to as

    A Dematerialisation
    B Immobilisation
    C Certificated form
    D Bearer form

17. An issue of free new shares to an existing shareholder in proportion to their existing holding, as at the record date, is known as a

    A Bonus issue
    B Scrip dividend
    C Rights issue
    D Return of capital

18. **SETS is available for trading in**

    A All ISDX Market shares
    B Only FTSE 350 shares
    C All AIM shares
    D All FTSE 100 shares

19. **Which of the following measures is used to determine whether a company's shares are included in the FTSE 100 Index?**

    A Market capitalisation
    B Net profit after tax
    C Turnover
    D Number of employees

20. **Which of the following is the primary criterion for determining the legal title of a share?**

    A Possession of a share certificate
    B Entry on register
    C Records of electronic holdings held by CREST (Euroclear UK & Ireland)
    D Contract note with details of trade

21. **A sells shares to B and the transaction takes place through CREST (Euroclear UK & Ireland, or EUI). How will the registrar be informed of the change of ownership in order to make the necessary amendments?**

    A A's bank will inform the registrar
    B B's bank will inform the registrar
    C CREST (EUI) will send an electronic message to the registrar
    D CREST (EUI) will send a share certificate and stock transfer form to the Registrar

22. **The primary purpose of issuing gilts is to**

    A To raise money for business
    B To fund government borrowing
    C To reduce the balance of payments
    D To reduce the National Debt

23. **An offset mortgage is a mortgage arrangement in which**

    A The mortgage is backed by a guarantor who agrees to make any payments on which the borrower defaults
    B The mortgage enables the borrower to erase any negative equity from an existing home owned
    C The mortgage debt balance is offset against positive account balances
    D Buy-to-let rental income is used to repay the mortgage

24. **A bond has a coupon of 7.5%. What will the price of the bond be if general interest rates are 6%?**

    A £80.00
    B £101.50
    C £115.00
    D £125.00

25. **Which of the following is the best definition of a future?**

    A A flexible contract where the investor buys and asset and agrees to sell it a future date
    B A flexible contract where the value is based on price movements of an underlying asset
    C A standardised contract where the holder has the right to buy an asset before an expiry date
    D A standardised contract where the holder agrees to buy or sell a specified issue at a specified price on a specified date

26. **An investor who opens a short position in a futures contract**

    A Is committed to buying the underlying asset at a pre-agreed price on a specified future date
    B Is committed to delivering the underlying asset in exchange selling the underlying asset at a pre-agreed price on a future date
    C Has the right but not an obligation to buy the underlying asset at a pre-agreed price on a future date
    D Has the right but not an obligation to sell the underlying asset at a pre-agreed price on a future date

27. **As a member of a professional body in the financial services industry, you have agreed to the Code of Ethics of that body. As an approved person, you are subject to the regulatory requirements. What is the best description of how you will act in an ethical manner?**

    A You will make sure that you have passed all appropriate examinations and that your approved person status is maintained
    B You will act in accordance with the wishes of your client at all times, above all else
    C You will act in accordance with your commitment to the highest standards of personal integrity in carrying out professional work
    D You will act in accordance with all of the regulator's rules on business conduct

28. **Which of the following is the main role of the manager of a unit trust?**

    A Making investment decisions
    B Safeguarding assets
    C Protecting the interests of investors
    D Creating and cancelling units

29. Which of the following would normally sell units in a unit trust?

   A Registrar
   B Trustee
   C Manager
   D Depository

30. From 2013/14, in what circumstances is the rate of inheritance tax is reduced from 40% to 36%?

   A For the portion of the estate between the nil rate band and £500,000
   B For estates that do not exceed £500,000
   C In cases where at least 10% of the estate is left to charity
   D In cases where at least 25% of the estate is left to charity

31. How is the price of an OEIC share set, under single pricing?

   A Bid price of underlying investments
   B Offer price of underlying investments
   C Mid-price of underlying investments
   D Estimated fair value of investments

32. What is meant by the term 'closed-ended' in relation to an investment trust?

   A Fund has a limited life
   B Share capital is fixed
   C Only institutional investors may purchase the fund
   D The fund invests in a fixed set of investments

33. What is the meaning of 'trading at a premium' in relation to an investment trust?

   A Share price is above net asset value
   B Share price is below net asset value
   C Price is based on net asset value with charges added
   D Price is based on net asset value with charges deducted

34. Which investment would best allow an investor to have an exposure to an ungeared fund investing in FTSE 100 stocks with a narrow bid-offer spread and real-time pricing?

   A An at-the-money FTSE 100 call option
   B An out-of-the-money FTSE 100 call option
   C A FTSE 100 exchange traded fund
   D A FTSE 100 tracker unit trust

35. **Which of the following is a type of fund often having an aggressive investment strategy taking advantage of arbitrage, short positions, futures and options and swaps?**

    A Hedge fund
    B Equity fund
    C Money market fund
    D Exchange traded fund

36. **A 'NURS' is a**

    A Non-regulated Undercapitalised Retail Scheme
    B Non-authorised Un-Regulated Scheme
    C Non-UCITS Un-Regulated Scheme
    D Non-UCITS Retail Scheme

37. **Which of the following are the three stages of money laundering?**

    A Inception, layering, separation
    B Initiation, integration, withdrawal
    C Placement, layering, integration
    D Inception, separation, withdrawal

38. **Which of the following would not normally be satisfactory evidence of the identity of an individual for money laundering purposes?**

    A Photographic driving licence
    B Electoral roll entry
    C Recent utility bill
    D National Insurance number

39. **Which of the following would be considered to be insider dealing?**

    A A director dealing on non-public price sensitive information
    B A director dealing during the three months prior to publication of the accounts
    C A director dealing in the shares of an associate company
    D A director dealing in any closed period for the shares where this is part of a regular commitment to purchase

40. **Which of the following is a principal objective of the Data Protection Act?**

    A To ensure that information on individuals is kept for no longer than one year
    B To ensure that companies do not release price-sensitive information
    C To ensure that information on individuals is accurate and up-to-date
    D To ensure that the correct information is included in the financial statements of the company concerned

41. A financial adviser has received a written complaint from a client. The adviser deals with the complaint and advises the client that she can refer the matter to the Financial Ombudsman Service (FOS) if she is unsatisfied with the response. How much time does the complainant have to refer the matter to FOS?

    A   Five working days
    B   Four weeks
    C   Eight weeks
    D   Six months

42. How much would an investor receive from the Financial Services Compensation Scheme if he incurred a loss of £65,000 in investments following the insolvency of an authorised firm?

    A   £45,000
    B   £50,000
    C   £58,500
    D   £65,000

43. How old must an individual be to open a stocks and shares ISA in their own name?

    A   15
    B   16
    C   17
    D   18

44. In relation to purchasing a house, 'loan to value' is a measure of

    A   The extent of part ownership of the property
    B   The size of the mortgage loan in relation to the value of the property purchased
    C   The loan sought by the home buyer relative to the amount authorised by the lender
    D   The ratio of the lender's valuation of the house to the price offered or paid by the home buyer

45. What is the maximum charge under a newly opened stakeholder pension plan?

    A   1% of bid/offer spread
    B   £1 per month
    C   1.5% of fund value
    D   £100 per annum

46. Which of the following will be subject to capital gains on disposal?

    A   Gilts
    B   Principal residence
    C   Private car
    D   Options

47. Which of the following will not be subject to income tax?

    A Dividend income
    B Sale of shares
    C Interest on bonds
    D Interest on bank accounts

48. Who is the legal owner of assets in a trust?

    A Settlor
    B Trustee
    C Beneficiary
    D Remaindermen

49. How is an ISA mortgage most accurately described?

    A Lifetime
    B Repayment
    C Interest-only
    D Pension-linked

50. What type of policy is a whole of life policy which has a sum assured of £120,000 throughout the term of the policy?

    A Non-profit
    B Traditional with-profit
    C Unitised with-profit
    D Unit-linked

Answers

1. **C** An investment bank has the primary purpose of raising finance for businesses. Securities houses do this amongst many other functions

    BPP Study Text Chapter 1 Section 3.3 / CISI Workbook Chapter 1 Section 2

2. **B** Spot currency trades settle T + 2

    BPP Study Text Chapter 1 Section 7.2 / CISI Workbook Chapter 3 Section 3

3. **A** The flat yield is calculated as follows

    $$\text{Flat yield} = \frac{\text{Gross coupon}}{\text{Market price}} \times 100$$

    $$= \frac{£8}{£106} \times 100$$

    $$= 7.5\%$$

    BPP Study Text Chapter 2 Section 9.7 / CISI Workbook Chapter 5 Section 5.2

4. **A** Credit creation increases the money supply

    BPP Study Text Chapter 1 Section 1.7 / CISI Workbook Chapter 2 Section 4.1

5. **D** The balance of payments is a measure of imports and exports

    BPP Study Text Chapter 1 Section 1.9.3 / CISI Workbook Chapter 2 Section 5.2.3

6. **B** The FPC and MPC are committees of the Bank of England. The PRA is a subsidiary of the Bank of England. The Bank has a significantly wider role in regulation since the 2013 re-structuring of the regulatory system

    BPP Study Text Chapter 1 Section 2.2 / CISI Workbook Chapter 2 Section 3.2

7. **D** CIC can be taken out to provide lump sum cover

    BPP Study Text Chapter 4 Section 7 / CISI Workbook Chapter 10 Section 3.3

8. **D** Increase in inflation is the most likely effect of an increase in PSNCR since the government, via the DMO, issues gilts to fund the PSNCR and then the money borrowed money leads to increased money supply and inflation

    BPP Study Text Chapter 1 Section 1.8 and Chapter 2 Section 8.3 / CISI Workbook Chapter 2 Section 5.2.4

9. **C** Interest rates tend to be higher on fixed term deposits rather than instant access

    BPP Study Text Chapter 4 Section 1 / CISI Workbook Chapter 3 Section 2

10. **A** Money market instruments are generally seen to service the short-term wholesale cash market

    BPP Study Text Chapter 2 Section 10.1 / CISI Workbook Chapter 3 Section 3

11.	A	Many institutional investors avoid residential property, although there are some funds that specialise in this area
		BPP Study Text Chapter 4 Section 2.1 / CISI Workbook Chapter 3 Section 4
12.	A	CAC 40 is the main French index
		BPP Study Text Chapter 2 Section 5.2 / CISI Workbook Chapter 4 Section 9.1
13.	C	Shares in private companies may not be sold to the public
		BPP Study Text Chapter 2 Section 1.1 / CISI Workbook Chapter 4 Section 7.2
14.	D	Anybody can put money into a Junior ISA – not just parents or other relatives
		BPP Study Text Chapter 7 Section 7.4 / CISI Workbook Chapter 9 Section 3.2
15.	B	Smaller, growing companies tend to list on AIM
		BPP Study Text Chapter 2 Section 4.3 / CISI Workbook Chapter 4 Section 7.2.2
16.	A	Where stock is held in uncertificated (electronic) form, this is called 'dematerialisation'. 'Immobilisation' involves share certificates being held in a depository
		BPP Study Text Chapter 2 Section 2.8 / CISI Workbook Chapter 4 Section 11
17.	A	Free shares *pro rata* to the existing holding comprise a bonus issue
		BPP Study Text Chapter 2 Section 3.2 / CISI Workbook Chapter 4 Section 6
18.	D	All FTSE 100 shares are quoted on SETS as are all FTSE 350 shares. However, the key word here is 'only' which makes the phrase 'only FTSE 350 shares' incorrect
		BPP Study Text Chapter 2 Section 6.2.1 / CISI Workbook Chapter 4 Section 10.1
19.	A	Market capitalisation is the qualifying criterion for entry into FTSE 100
		BPP Study Text Chapter 2 Section 5.2 / CISI Workbook Chapter 4 Section 9.1
20.	B	Entry on the company register of shareholders is used to determine legal title to shares
		BPP Study Text Chapter 2 Section 7.4.6 / CISI Workbook Chapter 4 Section 11
21.	C	CREST (Euroclear UK & Ireland) will send an RUR (Register Update Request) to the registrar to initiate the update of the register
		BPP Study Text Chapter 2 Section 7.6 / CISI Workbook Chapter 4 Section 13
22.	B	Gilts are a method used to fund government borrowing
		BPP Study Text Chapter 2 Section 8.1 / CISI Workbook Chapter 5 Section 3
23.	C	With what is normally known as an offset mortgage, for the purpose of calculation of interest charged, the mortgage balance is offset against, for example, savings and/or current account balances the homebuyer may hold
		BPP Study Text Chapter 4 Section 6.3 / CISI Workbook Chapter 10 Section 2.4.3

24.	D	Coupon is higher than general interest rates so the bond will be priced above par (above £100). At a price of £125 the yield is 6% which is the same as the general rate

BPP Study Text Chapter 2 Section 9.7 / CISI Workbook Chapter 5 Section 5.2

25.	D	Futures are standardised and have a specified date and price

BPP Study Text Chapter 3 Section 2.1 / CISI Workbook Chapter 6 Section 2

26.	B	A 'short' position is the opening position taken by someone who sells the futures contract

BPP Study Text Chapter 3 Section 2.2 / CISI Workbook Chapter 6 Section 2.3

27.	C	Exam passes and approved person status do not make you act ethically (Option A). Sometimes other legal requirements, such as to report suspicions of financial crime, must override your duty to a client, including the duty to act with confidentiality (Option B). Acting ethically involves more than compliance with rules (Option D)

BPP Study Text Chapter 6 Section 7.8 / CISI Workbook Chapter 8 Section 7.6

28.	A	Most significantly, the manager makes investment decisions for the fund

BPP Study Text Chapter 5 Section 2.1 / CISI Workbook Chapter 7 Section 2

29.	C	The manager ensures that there is a market by buying and selling the units

BPP Study Text Chapter 5 Section 2.1 / CISI Workbook Chapter 7 Section 2

30.	C	The reduced rate applies in cases where at least 10% of the estate is left to charity

BPP Study Text Chapter 7 Section 3.1 / CISI Workbook Chapter 9 Section 2.3

31.	C	OEICs are most commonly single-priced, based on the mid-value of the underlying investments

BPP Study Text Chapter 5 Section 3.2 / CISI Workbook Chapter 7 Section 4

32.	B	The share capital is fixed

BPP Study Text Chapter 5 Section 4.1 / CISI Workbook Chapter 7 Section 5

33.	A	Share price is above NAV, reflecting strong demand for the IT

BPP Study Text Chapter 5 Section 4.2 / CISI Workbook Chapter 7 Section 5

34.	C	The answer cannot refer to options, since they are geared – in this case, permitting the magnification of profits or losses through investment of the premium. The narrow bid-offer spread indicates an exchange traded fund rather than a unit trust

BPP Study Text Chapter 5 Section 5 / CISI Workbook Chapter 7 Section 7

35.	A	Hedge funds tend to use the investment strategies mentioned in the question

BPP Study Text Chapter 5 Section 6 / CISI Workbook Chapter 7 Section 9

36.	D	There are not many NURSs, which are retail schemes that do not comply with all of the UCITS conditions

BPP Study Text Chapter 5 Section 2.3 / CISI Workbook Chapter 7 Section 1.5.2

Introduction to Securities and Investment ♦ Practice Examination 3 – Answers

37. **C** Placement, layering and integration are the three stages of money laundering

BPP Study Text Chapter 6 Section 2.2 / CISI Workbook Chapter 8 Section 2.1.1

38. **D** Presentation of a national insurance number arguably does not provide sufficient evidence of identity

BPP Study Text Chapter 6 Section 2.8 / CISI Workbook Chapter 8 Section 2.1.3

39. **A** Dealing on non-public price-sensitive information is the definition of insider dealing

BPP Study Text Chapter 6 Section 3.2 / CISI Workbook Chapter 8 Section 3

40. **C** Information must be kept accurate and up-to-date

BPP Study Text Chapter 6 Section 4 / CISI Workbook Chapter 8 Section 5

41. **D** A complainant should normally refer the matter to FOS within six months since the firm sent its a final response

BPP Study Text Chapter 6 Section 5.1 / CISI Workbook Chapter 8 Section 6.3

42. **B** For investments, 100% × £50,000 = £50,000

BPP Study Text Chapter 6 Section 5.3 / CISI Workbook Chapter 8 Section 6.4

43. **D** An investor must be aged at least 18 (and UK-resident) to open a stocks and shares ISA

BPP Study Text Chapter 7 Section 7.1 / CISI Workbook Chapter 9 Section 3.1

44. **B** The LTV ratio is the size of the loan in relation to the value of the property purchased

BPP Study Text Chapter 4 Section 6.1 / CISI Workbook Chapter 10 Section 2.2

45. **C** 1.5% is the maximum charge on a newly opened stakeholder pension plan

BPP Study Text Chapter 4 Section 3.6 / CISI Workbook Chapter 9 Section 4.6

46. **D** If there is no specific exemption, disposal of an asset is generally chargeable to CGT. A sale of options would be subject to CGT, while the other choices are all exempt

BPP Study Text Chapter 7 Section 2.2 / CISI Workbook Chapter 9 Section 2.2

47. **B** The sale of shares is potentially liable to CGT. All the others are forms of income, and hence subject to Income Tax

BPP Study Text Chapter 7 Sections 1 and 2 / CISI Workbook Chapter 9 Section 2.1

48. **B** The trustee is the legal owner of assets in the trust

BPP Study Text Chapter 7 Section 8.2 / CISI Workbook Chapter 9 Section 6

49. **C** With an ISA mortgage, the ISA is available for eventual repayment of the capital of the mortgage, on which interest only is paid until repayment of the mortgage

BPP Study Text Chapter 4 Section 6.2 and Chapter 7 Section 7 / CISI Workbook Chapter 10 Section 2.4.2

50. **A** Non-profit policies have a fixed sum assured

BPP Study Text Chapter 4 Section 7 / CISI Workbook Chapter 10 Section 3.1

Practice Examination 4

50 Questions in 1 Hour

1. **What does the S&P 500 index most closely represent?**

   A A broad view of the US equity market

   B A narrow view of the US equity market

   C A broad view of the US commodity markets

   D A narrow view of the US commodity markets

2. **Fixed interest securities generally entitle the owner to**

   A Regular interest payments

   B A vote at the AGM of the issuing company

   C A right to dividend payments

   D Repayment of the price paid for the security

3. **Which of the following areas is covered by the Companies Act 2006?**

   A Insider dealing

   B Listing rules

   C Money laundering

   D Protection of shareholders from abuses of power by directors

4. **Which of the following is not specifically mentioned in the FCA's eleven Principles for Businesses?**

   A Skill, care and diligence

   B Relations with regulators

   C Unreasonable charging

   D Conflicts of interest

5. **What instrument gives a buyer the right, but not the obligation, to buy the underlying equity at a specified date in the future?**

   A A future

   B A call

   C A forward

   D A put

6. **What is the effect on the value of an investor's portfolio of a bonus issue?**

   A The portfolio will fall in value
   B The portfolio will rise in value
   C The portfolio will be unchanged
   D An indeterminate effect

7. **Which of the following statements best describes a rights issue?**

   A A free issue of shares to existing shareholders in proportion to their existing holding
   B An issue of shares to existing shareholders in proportion to their existing holding at a predetermined price
   C An issue of shares to existing shareholders in proportion to their existing holding at the current market price
   D An issue of shares to the market at a predetermined price

8. **Which of the following statements regarding indices is false?**

   A The Dow Jones Industrial Average represents 50 top US companies
   B The Nikkei Dow represents 225 Japanese companies
   C The DAX represents the 30 leading German companies
   D Investors use indices for benchmarking purposes

9. **The earliest age at which a pension-linked mortgage can normally be repaid using the pension plan proceeds is currently**

   A 50
   B 55
   C 60
   D 65

10. **The FTSE 250 index covers**

    A The 250 best performing companies in the UK
    B The largest 250 companies listed on the LSE weighted by market capitalisation
    C The next 250 companies listed on the LSE weighted by market capitalisation after the companies in the FTSE 100
    D The full list of AIM companies

11. **In the UK, equity trades normally settle on a timescale of**

    A T + 1
    B T + 2
    C T + 3
    D T + 4

12. Which of the following investments would not have capital gains tax applied to a trading gain when sold?

   A Gold
   B Gilts
   C Stamp collection
   D Shares

13. Which of the following is a 'closed-ended' form of investment?

   A Unit trusts
   B Investment trusts
   C OEICs
   D Unit trust ISAs

14. Which of the following are quoted companies that are set up for the purpose of investing in the shares of other companies?

   A Unit trusts
   B Investment trusts
   C OEICs
   D Unit trust ISAs

15. The date shown on a share certificate will be

   A The trade date
   B The settlement date
   C The date of transfer effected by the registrar
   D Two weeks after trade date

16. When will a foreign exchange deal struck on Monday normally settle?

   A Tuesday
   B Wednesday
   C Thursday
   D Friday

17. If a developed economy experiences a high level of inflation, which of the following is the most likely result?

   A Increased certainty as to the value of personal investments
   B Balance of payments surplus
   C Loss of international competitiveness
   D Higher taxation

18. Which of the following is the best definition of money laundering?

    A Making shareholder profits by using information not in the public domain
    B The process by which criminals attempt to hide the true origin of the proceeds of criminal activities
    C Trading in multiple small parcels of shares to disguise the purchase of a holding in excess of 3%
    D Directors trading in the shares of a company within one month of the publication of company results

19. What is another commonly used name for the ordinary shares of public limited companies?

    A Gilts
    B Warrants
    C Equities
    D Futures

20. Which of the following would not be a reason for owning a conventional gilt?

    A To receive regular interest income payments
    B To receive a guaranteed redemption value
    C To achieve better diversification of a portfolio
    D To gain more interest income on the gilt as general interest rates rise

21. What term most accurately describes the fixed income return earned from a bond?

    A Dividend
    B Yield
    C Coupon
    D Return

22. Which of the following indices represents the highest proportion of the relevant country's market capitalisation?

    A FTSE All Share
    B FTSE 100
    C S&P 500
    D Nikkei 225

23. Which of the following would be the most likely reason to own shares instead of fixed income instruments?

    A To receiving voting rights and guaranteed, regular income
    B To receive guaranteed, regular income and a redemption value after ten years
    C To receiving voting rights and potential capital appreciation
    D To receiving guaranteed, regular income and the right of first refusal to new shares in the company

24. For unit trusts, which of the following are duties of the investment manager?

    I   Safeguarding the assets
    II Investing the assets
    III Pricing the units
    IV Being the legal owner of the assets

    A I and II only
    B I, II and III only
    C II and IV only
    D II and III only

25. Which of the following roles must be performed by an LSE member firm?

    A Funds management
    B Market making
    C Mergers and acquisitions
    D Futures trading

26. Which of the following is the most likely role for an investment bank to fulfil?

    A Credit provision
    B Mergers and acquisitions
    C Global custody
    D Stock lending

27. Calculate the total net interest payment received by a higher rate (40%) taxpayer who deposits £10,000 in a bank account yielding 5% per annum over four years.

    A £400
    B £500
    C £1,600
    D £2,000

28. Which pension option for the member of a defined contribution scheme presents the greatest risk that the monetary amount of pension paid could fall?

    A Income drawdown
    B Lifetime annuity
    C Scheme pension
    D Open market option annuity

29. Which of the following cannot be a type of unit trust?

    A UCITS fund
    B A non-retail UCITS retail scheme
    C A qualified investor scheme
    D Exchange-traded fund

30. **Which of the following organises the issuance of UK government bonds?**

    A   The Bank of England
    B   London Stock Exchange
    C   Debt Management Office
    D   NYSE Liffe

31. **Which one of the following types of risk does not contribute to credit risk?**

    A   Interest rate risk
    B   Issuer risk
    C   Counterparty risk
    D   Settlement risk

32. **Which of the following statements is true with regard to the Financial Services Compensation Scheme (FSCS)?**

    A   The FSCS will adjudicate in a dispute between a consumer and an authorised firm
    B   The FCSC is unable to make payments in the event that a firm becomes insolvent
    C   The FSCS is accountable to the FCA and HM Treasury
    D   The FSCS provides for compensation of up to £150,000 to be paid per claim

33. **Which of the following is a benefit of a company being quoted on the LSE? (Choose the most appropriate answer.)**

    A   The ability to pay dividends annually
    B   The requirement to report on a regular basis
    C   The ability to use newly issued shares to purchase the shares of companies being taken over
    D   The ability to market products to the public

34. **Which of the following types of organisation is involved in most directly credit creation?**

    A   Central banks
    B   Insurance companies
    C   Commercial banks
    D   Stock brokers

35. **The stage of money laundering in which money from an illegal source is mingled with money from a legitimate source is described as**

    A   Dissemination
    B   Integration
    C   Layering
    D   Placement

36. **Which of the following has as its central aim the creation of a single market in financial services across Europe?**

    A   The Financial Services Action Plan
    B   The Financial Services and Markets Act
    C   The Financial Policy Committee
    D   The Prudential Regulation Authority

37. **Which trading platform would you probably be using for trading a share that has low liquidity?**

    A   SETS
    B   SETSqx
    C   CoredealMTS
    D   CREST (Euroclear UK & Ireland)

38. **Which one of the following would mean that the offence of insider dealing has been committed?**

    A   Dealing without the intention of making a profit
    B   Dealing on information you believed was generally available
    C   Dealing, despite the information known, in order to settle a debt
    D   Dealing on information that is not available to the general public

39. **What is normally the maximum lifespan of Commercial Paper?**

    A   30 days
    B   90 days
    C   180 days
    D   365 days

40. **Customer functions differ from other controlled functions in the respect that customer function personnel**

    A   Must comply with significant influence function requirements
    B   Are required to be approved persons
    C   Are not required to be approved persons
    D   Are not subject to significant influence function requirements

41. **Which of the following is not true of market abuse?**

    A   It is a civil offence
    B   The maximum penalty is seven years in jail and an unlimited fine
    C   It may relate to trading based on unavailable information
    D   It relates to trading in qualifying investments on a prescribed market

42. Which of the following is a chief reason for the issuance of gilts?

    A To ensure that there is a strong cash flow within the UK economy
    B To provide investors with a higher return when interest rates are low
    C To fund government spending in excess of receipts
    D To ensure that there is a high level of central reserves

43. What is the main advantage of a derivative being exchange-traded?

    A The exchange guarantees that settlement will take place
    B The derivative is custom made for client needs
    C There is no margin requirement for either party to the transaction
    D Such derivatives can be arranged for all securities

44. A bullish investor opening a position in the June FTSE future is described as being

    A Long
    B Short
    C Flat
    D In the money

45. Which of the following is the best description with regard to GDP?

    A It represents the value of all activities paid for in cash and other financial activities
    B It is the goods and services produced within an economy
    C A rising GDP will indicate a falling standard of living
    D It will include black market activity

46. The age at which a child can withdraw funds from a Junior ISA is normally

    A 14
    B 16
    C 18
    D 21

47. A convertible bond is so called normally because it is

    A Redeemable in more than one currency
    B A derivative that is generally settled in cash
    C Convertible to equity
    D Convertible to a zero coupon bond

48. **Which of the following is the best description of a takeover?**

    A The management buying out the shareholders of a company
    B One company buying out another company
    C The liquidation of a company
    D Shareholders voting to remove the Chief Executive of a company

49. **Where is the main legislation regarding market abuse to be found?**

    A Financial Services and Markets Act 2000
    B UKLA Listing Rules
    C Criminal Justice Act 1993
    D Proceeds of Crime Act 2002

50. **Which of the following is the best description of insider trading?**

    A Making profits from share trading by using information not in the public domain
    B The process by which criminals attempt to hide the true origin of the proceeds of criminal activities
    C Trading in multiple small packets of shares to disguise the purchase of a holding in excess of 3%
    D Directors trading in the shares of a company within one month of the publication of company results

Answers

1. **A** The S&P 500 is broader than the Dow Jones Industrial Average, which only covers 30 US shares

   BPP Study Text Chapter 2 Section 5.2 / CISI Workbook Chapter 4 Section 9

2. **A** It is equity shareholders who have the right to vote and receive dividends, if the company pays them. Fixed interest securities will generally entitle the bondholder to repayment of the par (nominal) value on redemption

   BPP Study Text Chapter 2 Sections 8.1 and 9.1 / CISI Workbook Chapter 5 Section 2

3. **D** Insider trading, listing and money laundering are each covered by specific legislation

   BPP Study Text Chapter 2 Section 1.1 / CISI Workbook Chapter 8 Section 2

4. **C** Firms should treat customers 'fairly', but unreasonable charging is not mentioned

   BPP Study Text Chapter 6 Sections 1.5 / CISI Workbook Chapter 8 Section 1.3

5. **B** The right to buy is a call option, an obligation to buy would be a long future

   BPP Study Text Chapter 3 Section 3.1 / CISI Workbook Chapter 6 Section 3

6. **C** Remember that a bonus issue is used by companies to improve liquidity by spreading the value of the company among a greater number of shares. Existing shareholders are given new shares, completely free. Thus, while the individual share price will be lower, the portfolio still has the same overall value

   BPP Study Text Chapter 2 Section 3.2 / CISI Workbook Chapter 4 Section 6

7. **B** Existing shareholders have pre-emption rights (a right of first refusal), allowing them to take up the offer and purchase new shares at the predetermined subscription price

   BPP Study Text Chapter 2 Section 3.3 / CISI Workbook Chapter 4 Section 6

8. **A** The Dow Jones covers 30 US companies

   BPP Study Text Chapter 2 Section 5.2 / CISI Workbook Chapter 4 Section 9

9. **B** Repayment of the mortgage is made from the tax-free cash paid on retirement out of a pension plan. Pension benefits may be taken from age 55 under HMRC rules

   BPP Study Text Chapter 4 Section 3.5 / CISI Workbook Chapter 10 Section 2.2

10. **C** The FTSE 250 Index comprises the shares of the 250 largest companies after the top 100 companies listed on the LSE

    BPP Study Text Chapter 2 Section 5.2 / CISI Workbook Chapter 4 Section 9.1

11. **C** T + 3 means within three business days after the transaction

    BPP Study Text Chapter 2 Section 7.2 / CISI Workbook Chapter 4 Section 13

12. **B** Gains on the disposal of gilts are exempt from CGT

    BPP Study Text Chapter 7 Section 2.2 / CISI Workbook Chapter 9 Section 2.2

Introduction to Securities and Investment ♦ Practice Examination 4 – Answers

13. **B** Investment trusts close for subscription after their launch. Their value then tracks the value of the funds invested

    BPP Study Text Chapter 5 Section 4.1 / CISI Workbook Chapter 7 Section 5

14. **B** Investment trusts are quoted companies priced on the LSE

    BPP Study Text Chapter 5 Section 4.1 / CISI Workbook Chapter 7 Section 5

15. **C** It is only when the registrar has amended the share register that the buyer of the shares becomes the new legal owner and enjoys all the rights and privileges that accompany being a shareholder

    BPP Study Text Chapter 2 Section 2.8.1 / CISI Workbook Chapter 4 Section 11

16. **B** Spot forex transactions normally settle T + 2, so a deal struck on Monday will settle on Wednesday. This is a tricky question since it does not specify whether we are dealing with spot or forward trades

    BPP Study Text Chapter 1 Section 7.2 / CISI Workbook Chapter 3 Section 5

17. **C** This is the best answer available. There are, of course, many other likely consequences of inflation, including erosion of the value of personal investments

    BPP Study Text Chapter 1 Section 1.8 / CISI Workbook Chapter 2 Section 4

18. **B** This is a good definition of money laundering

    BPP Study Text Chapter 6 Section 3.1 / CISI Workbook Chapter 8 Section 2.1

19. **C** Shares are also known as equity investments

    BPP Study Text Chapter 2 Section 2.1 / CISI Workbook Chapter 4 Section 3.1

20. **D** A 'conventional' gilt is not an index-linked gilt. When the Debt Management Office issues a conventional gilt, the coupon (which determines the amount of interest income that will be received) is fixed. Only a floating rate instrument will offer additional interest income if general interest rates rise

    BPP Study Text Chapter 2 Section 8.2 / CISI Workbook Chapter 5 Section 3.1.1

21. **C** Dividend for equities; coupons for bonds

    BPP Study Text Chapter 2 Section 8.1 / CISI Workbook Chapter 5 Section 2

22. **A** The FTSE 100 is an index of the top 100 UK public companies by market capitalisation, while the FTSE All Share is an index of all listed companies. The FTSE All Share represents approximately 98% of the UK market by value

    BPP Study Text Chapter 2 Section 5.2 / CISI Workbook Chapter 4 Section 9

23. **C** Ordinary shares carry voting rights but no legal right to receive a dividend. However, ordinary shareholders will share equally in a dividend, should one be declared by a company

    BPP Study Text Chapter 2 Section 2 / CISI Workbook Chapter 4 Section 4

24. **D** The investment manager is responsible for trading the assets and pricing the units. The trustee looks after the issuance of new units and is the legal owner of the assets

    BPP Study Text Chapter 5 Section 2.1 / CISI Workbook Chapter 7 Section 2

Introduction to Securities and Investment ♦ Practice Examination 4 – Answers

25. **B** This is the best answer available, as some LSE members also manage funds. The key point to note is that you cannot be a market maker without being an LSE member, whereas fund managers do not have to be LSE members

    BPP Study Text Chapter 1 Sections 3.8 and 4.1 / CISI Workbook Chapter 4 Section 10

26. **B** Investment banks tend not to provide credit. Custody and stock lending are roles of the global custodian

    BPP Study Text Chapter 1 Section 3.3 / CISI Workbook Chapter 1 Section 2

27. **C** The total net interest payment = £10,000 × 5% = £500 p.a., thus £2,000 over the four years

    Remember that banks and building societies will deduct 20% withholding tax (or the basic rate of tax on interest income) at source. Thus

    £2,000 × (1 – tax rate) = £1,600

    Further, the investor will be liable to pay a further 20%

    BPP Study Text Chapter 4 Section 1 / CISI Workbook Chapter 3 Section 2

28. **A** With income drawdown, the fund could be depleted by poor investment performance, leading to a fall in the amount that can be withdrawn as income. Income from an annuity or scheme pension will not decline in this way. The open market option is the ability of the investor to choose from various annuity providers

    BPP Study Text Chapter 4 Section 3.3.3 / CISI Workbook Chapter 9 Section 4.8

29. **D** Unit trusts are not exchange-traded; units are traded via the fund manager

    BPP Study Text Chapter 5 Section 2.3 / CISI Workbook Chapter 7 Sections 2 and 7

30. **C** The Debt Management Office is the full name. The DMO is an agency of the Treasury

    BPP Study Text Chapter 2 Section 8.3 / CISI Workbook Chapter 5 Section 3.3

31. **A** Issuer risk, counterparty risk and settlement risk are all components of credit risk

    BPP Study Text Chapter 2 Section 2.7 / CISI Workbook Chapter 5 Section 5.3

32. **C** The Financial Ombudsman Service is the body responsible for adjudication of disputes. The maximum compensation for claims against firms declared in default is 100% of the first £50,000 per person per claim for investments, and £85,000 for bank deposits

    BPP Study Text Chapter 6 Section 6.3 / CISI Workbook Chapter 8 Section 1.2.1

33. **C** The only definite advantage from among the options given is the ability to use shares to finance the takeover of target companies

    BPP Study Text Chapter 2 Section 4.1 / CISI Workbook Chapter 4 Section 7.2

34. **C** The creation of credit can be achieved by the 'recycling' of funds placed on deposit with banks

    BPP Study Text Chapter 1 Section 1.7 / CISI Workbook Chapter 2 Section 4.1

35. **C** In the 'layering' phase of money laundering, the original source of funds is disguised

    BPP Study Text Chapter 6 Section 2.3 / CISI Workbook Chapter 8 Section 2.1.1

36. **A** The FSAP is a EU initiative with this aim. The other options are UK institutions or legislation

    BPP Study Text Chapter 6 Section 1.3 / CISI Workbook Chapter 8 Section 1.2

Introduction to Securities and Investment ♦ Practice Examination 4 – Answers

37.	B	Liquid shares trade on SETS. CREST is a settlement system, not a trading platform
		BPP Study Text Chapter 2 Section 6.5.1 / CISI Workbook Chapter 4 Section 10.1
38.	D	Insider dealing is trading on information that is not publicly available
		BPP Study Text Chapter 6 Section 4.2 / CISI Workbook Chapter 8 Section 3
39.	D	Commercial paper can have a lifespan of between eight and 365 days
		BPP Study Text Chapter 2 Section 10.2 / CISI Workbook Chapter 3 Section 3
40.	D	Customer function personnel do not have to comply with the significant-influence requirements. All persons carrying out controlled functions must be approved persons
		BPP Study Text Chapter 6 Section 1.5 / CISI Workbook Chapter 8 Section 1.4
41.	B	Since market abuse is a civil offence, the guilty party cannot be sent to jail for it
		BPP Study Text Chapter 6 Section 4.3 / CISI Workbook Chapter 8 Section 4
42.	C	Gilts help to finance the spending of the Government in excess of tax revenues
		BPP Study Text Chapter 1 Section 1.9.3 / CISI Workbook Chapter 5 Section 3
43.	A	By means of a clearing house, the exchange guarantees that the transaction will settle. The range of derivatives available will be limited to whatever the exchange offers
		BPP Study Text Chapter 3 Section 1 / CISI Workbook Chapter 6 Section 1
44.	A	A transaction in which a future is purchased to open a position is known as a long position
		BPP Study Text Chapter 3 Section 2.2 / CISI Workbook Chapter 6 Section 2.3
45.	B	GDP is a measure of the value of all goods and service produced in an economy
		BPP Study Text Chapter 1 Section 1.9.1 / CISI Workbook Chapter 2 Section 5.2.1
46.	C	The child can choose to become the registered contact for their JISA from age 16 and can withdraw money from age 18, when the Junior ISA converts to an ISA
		BPP Study Text Chapter 7 Section 7.4 / CISI Workbook Chapter 9 Section 3.2
47.	C	Such a bond is normally convertible to equity
		BPP Study Text Chapter 2 Section 9.6 / CISI Workbook Chapter 5 Section 4.2.5
48.	C	A company seeking to expand may either grow organically or by buying other companies. In a takeover, one company acquires another company
		BPP Study Text Chapter 2 Section 3.5 / CISI Workbook Chapter 4 Section 6.5
49.	A	FSMA 2000 s118 contains the legislation regarding market abuse
		BPP Study Text Chapter 6 Section 4.3 / CISI Workbook Chapter 8 Section 4
50.	A	This is an appropriate definition of insider trading
		BPP Study Text Chapter 6 Section 4.1 / CISI Workbook Chapter 8 Section 3

Practice Examination 5

50 Questions in 1 Hour

1. What is the correct term for the risk that shares may be difficult to sell at a reasonable price or traded quickly enough in the market to prevent a loss?

   A Credit risk
   B Issuer risk
   C Price risk
   D Liquidity risk

2. On which of the following trading systems do FTSE 100 stocks trade?

   A SETS
   B IOB
   C SETSqx
   D NASDAQ

3. An investor bought £4,000 nominal value 5% Treasury stock for £3,900. Ignoring tax, how much is due for the next semi-annual interest payment?

   A £66.76
   B £100.00
   C £200.00
   D £300.00

4. Which of the following is not an advantage of there being a central counterparty in the process of clearing and settlement?

   A Enhanced trading liquidity
   B Dematerialisation of trades
   C Reduced risk for traders
   D Operational efficiencies

5. What percentage of those voting must vote in favour for a special resolution to be passed?

   A 50%
   B 55%
   C 75%
   D 80%

6. **Which of the following is not a form of tax-efficient saving for a higher rate taxpayer?**

   A Whole-of-life policy
   B Stakeholder pension plan
   C Equity ISA
   D Cash ISA

7. **An institutional investor Y plc enters into a credit default swap (CDS) in order to gain protection from the risk of a credit default by X plc, a company issuing debt securities. Which of the following events will not normally be one of the events which might be specified as triggering a payment to the CDS buyer?**

   A Restructuring of the debt securities of X plc
   B Change in the credit rating of Y plc
   C Insolvency of X plc
   D Failure to pay interest on the debt securities

8. **Which of the following is true of the process by which UK interest rates are set?**

   A Interest rates are set by the Monetary Policy Committee, in line with the European Central Bank's interest rate policy
   B Interest rates are set by the Monetary Policy Committee after considering inflation targets set by the Government
   C Interest rates are set by the Government
   D Interest rates are set by the Debt Management Office

9. **A major market for exchange-traded derivatives in the UK is**

   A ISDX
   B Euroclear
   C NYSE Liffe
   D LCH.Clearnet

10. **Who is responsible for the safekeeping of assets in an OEIC?**

    A Depositary
    B Authorised Corporate Director
    C Trustee
    D Manager

11. **A contract that gives the holder the right to sell an underlying equity is known as a**

    A Call
    B Put
    C Future
    D Forward

12. **On which of the following markets are certain transactions most typically described as 'spot' transactions?**

    A Equities
    B Gilts
    C Foreign exchange
    D Derivatives

13. **Which of the following is not a right of ordinary shareholders in a company?**

    A To vote at company meetings
    B To receive dividends annually
    C First refusal when new shares are issued
    D To receive an equal claim on liquidation of a company, once all other claimants have been paid

14. **Breaches of the Data Protection Act 1998 are punishable by**

    A Six months' imprisonment and a £5,000 fine
    B Seven years' imprisonment and an unlimited fine
    C Unlimited fines
    D A maximum fine of £100,000 plus costs

15. **Which of the following types of behaviour is not included under the market abuse regime?**

    A Dealing based on unavailable information
    B Conduct likely to create a misleading impression in the market
    C Behaviour likely to distort the market
    D Abusing the right to transfer data to a country outside the EEA

16. **Which of the following is the minimum quote size for a market maker?**

    A Large market size
    B Normal market size
    C Smallest market size
    D Average market size

17. **According to the Debt Management Office classification, a gilt-edged security with nine years left to run until maturity is**

    A A medium gilt
    B A long gilt
    C A short gilt
    D A terminal gilt

18. **With whom would it normally be possible to deal in unit trust units?**

    A Trustee
    B Custodian
    C Intermediary
    D Directly with another investor

19. **All of the following are examples of tradeable fixed income securities, except**

    A Yankee bonds
    B Gilts
    C Convertible bonds
    D Premium bonds

20. **The term 'pre-emptive rights' describes**

    A Offering shares to new shareholders prior to their general market release
    B Offering existing shareholders the right to buy new shares before others
    C Offering directors of the company shares at a price below that charged to the general public
    D Offering shares to only those who have held shares since the initial launch by the company

21. **A bond is issued in a country other than that of the issuer is known as a**

    A Domestic bond
    B Strippable bond
    C Eurobond
    D Government bond

22. **The CPI is used to measure**

    A Changes in interest rates
    B Changes in prices
    C Value of sterling
    D Standard variable rate on mortgages

23. **Alice is an investor who is over 50 years old. Having invested half of the maximum allowed in a stocks and shares ISA this tax year 2013/14 (£5,760), she has decided to open a cash ISA. What is the maximum amount that Alice can invest in a cash ISA in the tax year 2013/14?**

    A Nil
    B £3,720
    C £5,760
    D £11,520

24. **Which of the following instruments are generally considered to be derivatives?**

    A Futures and forex
    B Futures and options
    C Options and forex
    D Options and convertibles

25. **Which of the following is not one of the consumer outcomes arising from treating customers fairly, as identified by the regulator?**

    A Products and services marketed and sold in the retail market are designed to meet the needs of identified consumer groups and are targeted accordingly
    B Consumers do not face unreasonable post-sale barriers imposed by firms to change product, switch provider, submit a claim, or make a complaint
    C A firm takes reasonable care to ensure the suitability of its advice and discretionary decisions for any consumer who is entitled to rely upon its judgement
    D Consumers are provided with clear information and are kept appropriately informed before, during and after the point of sale

26. **Which of the following bodies is responsible for the listing rules in the UK?**

    A Department for Business, Innovation and Skills
    B Financial Policy Committee
    C Prudential Regulation Authority
    D Financial Conduct Authority

27. **A loan may be secured or unsecured. Which of the following is generally a secured loan?**

    A Second mortgage
    B Bank overdraft
    C Charge card balance
    D Credit card balance

28. **Mr Patel is seeking a mortgage as a first-time buyer. He wishes to take advantage of falling interest rates if they occur, but also wishes to have some protection against the risk of rates rising. Which type of interest rate is likely to suit him best?**

    A Variable
    B Tracker
    C Collar
    D Capped

29. **Which one of the following statements is not correct?**

   A A Junior ISA allows a maximum of £9,000 to be invested over a three-year period
   B Interest paid by banks and building societies generally has tax deducted at source
   C Cash investments are low-risk investments
   D The earliest age at which a child can open a Junior ISA for themselves is age 16

30. **For a borrower wishing to know the cost of borrowing, which of the following rates provides the most useful information?**

   A Quoted rate
   B Negotiated rate
   C Effective annual rate
   D Annualised interest repayments

31. **The stage of money laundering that describes the process where the original source of funds is disguised is called**

   A Layering
   B Integration
   C Termination
   D Placement

32. **From which of the following markets was Euronext formed?**

   A Amsterdam, Brussels and Milan
   B Amsterdam, Brussels and Paris
   C Brussels, Paris and Frankfurt
   D Amsterdam, Brussels and Frankfurt

33. **In which of the following circumstances is a certificated security deemed to be delivered?**

   A By book entry transfer
   B The certificate and a signed transfer form are sent to the buyer
   C The signed stock transfer form is sent to the buyer
   D By confirming the details of the holding with the register

34. **Which of the following is exempt from capital gains tax on its disposal?**

   A Antiques
   B Cars
   C Stamp collection
   D Second home

35. **An investment trust has the main purpose of**
    - A Investing in all type of financial assets
    - B Securing a return through the use of hedging techniques
    - C Providing a growing level of income
    - D Investing in the shares of other companies

36. **Shares in investment trusts are purchased by an investor in a similar way to the purchase of**
    - A OEICs
    - B Equities
    - C Unit trusts
    - D Commodities

37. **How many shares make up the Xetra Dax Index?**
    - A 10
    - B 30
    - C 100
    - D 250

38. **Which of the following types of mortgage would probably be most suitable for a homebuyer who is expecting general interest rates to fall in the future?**
    - A ISA mortgage
    - B Unit-linked mortgage
    - C Endowment mortgage
    - D Variable rate repayment mortgage

39. **Calculate the flat yield on the following bond: Treasury 6% 2028, when it is trading at £120.**
    - A 5.0%
    - B 6.0%
    - C 5.5%
    - D 6.5%

40. **A trust is established which gives the income beneficiary of the trust the legal right to live in a property during her lifetime. On her death the property will be held for the benefit of the second class beneficiary. This form of trust is best described as a**
    - A Bare trust
    - B Simple trust
    - C Interest in possession trust
    - D Charitable trust

41. **Which of the following is not a characteristic of Treasury bills?**

    A Issued by Debt Management Office
    B Pay interest referenced to LIBOR notes
    C Normal maturity is 91 days
    D Sold in minimum denominations of £25,000

42. **The most likely reason why a company might enter into an interest rate swap is**

    A To hedge the risk involved in either a fixed or floating rate by accepting its opposite
    B To benefit from market volatility
    C To reduce the level of its borrowings
    D To smooth investment returns

43. **Wendy is told by her bank that tax will be deducted from gross interest due. The remaining amount is referred to as**

    A Real interest
    B Nominal interest
    C Deflated interest
    D Net interest

44. **An investor originally sells a long gilt future and three weeks later buys back the same contract. He is said to have**

    A Gone long
    B Exercised his option
    C Closed out his position
    D Engaged in a swap transaction

45. **If you want the opportunity for substantial capital growth in your investment, which one of the following would you be most likely to buy?**

    A Equities
    B Gilts
    C Preference shares
    D Options

46. **An traded share option is best described as**

    A Providing an obligation to buy or sell a quantity of a specific share at a prespecified price on a prespecified date
    B A futures contract with which there is no obligation to buy or sell at the maturity date
    C Providing a right to buy or sell a quantity of a specific share at a prespecified price on a prespecified date
    D A commitment to purchase a quantity of a specific share at a pre-specified price with settlement taking place on a predetermined date

47. An investor buys a gilt for £96.78 and holds it until maturity, when it redeems at £100. The investor has already used her annual exempt allowance for capital gains tax purposes. How much will the investor pay in capital gains tax?

   A Nil
   B £3.22
   C 18% or 28% of £3.22, depending on tax status
   D 20% or 40% of £3.22, depending on tax status

48. The period which runs from the 6 April in one year to the 5 April in the next is known as the

   A Financial year
   B Fiscal year
   C Accounting year
   D Calendar year

49. Who would normally report a suspicious transaction to the Serious Organised Crime Agency (to become the National Crime Agency)?

   A The employee directly
   B The MLRO of the firm
   C The firm's executive committee
   D The JMSLG after consulting with the firm's compliance department

50. An investor uses an approach that seeks unpopular or unfashionable stocks carrying a growth potential that mainly goes unnoticed. This approach is best described as

   A Contrarian investing
   B Value investing
   C High yield investing
   D Passive investing

Answers

1. **D**   This is a definition of liquidity risk

   BPP Study Text Chapter 2 Section 2.7 / CISI Workbook Chapter 4 Section 5

2. **A**   FTSE 100 stocks trade on SETS

   BPP Study Text Chapter 2 Section 6.2 / CISI Workbook Chapter 4 Section 10.1

3. **B**   The semi-annual payment is

   Nominal value × 5% × ½

   = £4,000 × 5% × ½

   = £100

   BPP Study Text Chapter 2 Section 8.2.4 / CISI Workbook Chapter 5 Section 2

4. **B**   Dematerialisation is not necessarily a feature that goes with a central counterparty service. The central counterparty is able to enhance efficiency and liquidity partly by netting trades and partly by streamlining clearing and settlement

   BPP Study Text Chapter 2 Section 6.6 / CISI Workbook Chapter 4 Section 12

5. **C**   75% of those voting must vote in favour

   BPP Study Text Chapter 2 Section 1.4 / CISI Workbook Chapter 4 Section 2.3

6. **A**   Tax relief is available on contributions (within limits) to pension plans. ISAs, whether cash or stocks and shares types, also carry tax reliefs

   BPP Study Text Chapter 4 Section 3.8 and Chapter 6 Section 1 / CISI Workbook Chapter 10 Section 3

7. **B**   Y plc is the company buying protection, and so its credit rating will not be one of the specified credit events

   BPP Study Text Chapter 3 Section 5.3 / CISI Workbook Chapter 6 Section 4.3

8. **B**   Interest rates are set independently by the MPC after considering the inflation target

   BPP Study Text Chapter 1 Section 2.1.3 / CISI Workbook Chapter 2 Section 3.2.1

9. **C**   Note that LCH.Clearnet and Euroclear are clearing houses rather than exchanges

   BPP Study Text Chapter 1 Section 5.1 / CISI Workbook Chapter 6 Section 5.2.1

10. **A**   A depositary performs the same function of safekeeping in an OEIC as the trustees of a unit trust. The Authorised Corporate Director is the manager of an OEIC

    BPP Study Text Chapter 5 Section 3.2 / CISI Workbook Chapter 7 Section 3

11. **B**   The right to sell an underlying equity is known as a put option

    BPP Study Text Chapter 3 Section 3.1 / CISI Workbook Chapter 6 Section 3.3

Introduction to Securities and Investment ♦ Practice Examination 5 – Answers

12. **C** Transactions on the foreign exchange market for immediate trades at the current price are called 'spot' transactions

    BPP Study Text Chapter 1 Section 7.2 / CISI Workbook Chapter 3 Section 5

13. **B** There is no automatic right to receive a dividend each year, but all ordinary shareholders will participate equally if a dividend is declared

    BPP Study Text Chapter 2 Section 2 / CISI Workbook Chapter 4 Section 4

14. **C** This would be a Crown Court sanction. The maximum fine in a Magistrates' Court would be £5,000

    BPP Study Text Chapter 6 Section 4 / CISI Workbook Chapter 8 Section 5

15. **D** Transferring data outside the EEA, unless that country has adequate protection of rights of data subjects, is a breach of data protection law (Data Protection Act 1998) and does not fall within the market abuse regime

    BPP Study Text Chapter 6 Sections 3.3 and 4 / CISI Workbook Chapter 8 Section 5

16. **B** Normal Market Size is the minimum size for which a market maker must provide a quote

    BPP Study Text Chapter 2 Section 2.8.1 / CISI Workbook Chapter 4 Section 10.1

17. **A** A medium-dated gilt is one with between seven and fifteen years to maturity, according to the DMO classifications

    BPP Study Text Chapter 2 Section 8.4 / CISI Workbook Chapter 5 Section 3.2

18. **C** You could place an order through an intermediary and they, in turn, would deal with the fund manager

    BPP Study Text Chapter 5 Section 2.5 / CISI Workbook Chapter 7 Section 2

19. **D** Premium Bonds are offered by National Savings & Investments and cannot be traded. All of the other instruments may be kept until maturity or sold on into the market

    BPP Study Text Chapter 2 Section 9 / CISI Workbook Chapter 5 Section 2

20. **B** It is the right of existing shareholders to be offered the rights shares issued by the company, prior to others

    BPP Study Text Chapter 2 Section 2.5 / CISI Workbook Chapter 4 Section 6.2

21. **C** Eurobonds are normally issued in a country other than that of the issuer. The currency of issue does not link to the country it is issued in

    BPP Study Text Chapter 2 Section 9.1 / CISI Workbook Chapter 5 Section 4.4

22. **B** The Consumer Price Index measures the increase in consumer prices and, therefore, price inflation

    BPP Study Text Chapter 1 Section 1.8.1 / CISI Workbook Chapter 2 Section 5.1

23. **C** The maximum that can be invested in a cash ISA is £5,760 for 2013/14

    BPP Study Text Chapter 3 Section 3.3 / CISI Workbook Chapter 9 Section 3.1

24.	B	Futures and options derive their value from an underlying asset and refer to a deferred delivery at a future date. Forex is a phrase used to describe foreign exchange and covers both spot or immediate transactions and forwards, which are similar in nature to futures

BPP Study Text Chapter 3 Section 1 / CISI Workbook Chapter 6 Section 1

25.	C	The regulator identified six desirable consumer outcomes as part of the TCF initiative. Rather than being an outcome for consumers, Statement C is a requirement of Principle for Businesses 9, in relation to how firms treat all customers

BPP Study Text Chapter 6 Section 5.4 / CISI Workbook Chapter 8 Section 6.5

26.	D	The UK Listing Authority (UKLA) is responsible as the Competent Authority, and this is part of the FCA

BPP Study Text Chapter 2 Section 4 / CISI Workbook Chapter 4 Section 7

27.	A	A mortgage, including a second mortgage, is secured against property

BPP Study Text Chapter 4 Sections 5 and 6 / CISI Workbook Chapter 10 Section 2.2

28.	D	A capped rate will put a ceiling on the rate, limiting the client's risk, while allowing him to benefit if rates fall below the cap

BPP Study Text Chapter 4 Section 6.4 / CISI Workbook Chapter 10 Section 2.4

29.	A	The yearly maximum that can be invested in a Junior ISA is £3,720 (2013/14)

BPP Study Text Chapter 7 Section 7.4 / CISI Workbook Chapter 9 Section 3.2

30.	C	The Effective Annual Rate takes into account any charges the borrower is likely to pay (excluding fees for going overdrawn)

BPP Study Text Chapter 4 Section 5 / CISI Workbook Chapter 10 Section 1.4

31.	A	Layering describes the process whereby money is moved around the financial system to try to hide its origin. Placement is when the money is first put in and Integration is when the money, now seemingly legitimate, is taken out

BPP Study Text Chapter 6 Section 3.2 / CISI Workbook Chapter 8 Section 3.1.1

32.	B	The Euronext market was formed from the exchanges of Amsterdam, Paris and Brussels. The Lisbon exchange is now also part of Euronext

BPP Study Text Chapter 1 Section 6.2 / CISI Workbook Chapter 4 Section 8.2.2

33.	B	Delivery occurs when the old share certificate and signed stock transfer form are completed by the seller

BPP Study Text Chapter 2 Section 7.6 / CISI Workbook Chapter 4 Section 11

34.	B	Cars – considered to be wasting assets – are exempt from CGT

BPP Study Text Chapter 7 Section 2.2 / CISI Workbook Chapter 9 Section 2.2

35.	D	Investment trusts invest in the shares of other companies

BPP Study Text Chapter 5 Section 4.1 / CISI Workbook Chapter 7 Section 5

Introduction to Securities and Investment ♦ Practice Examination 5 – Answers

36. **B** Shares in investment trusts are purchased in the same way as equities, since both are quoted on the LSE

    BPP Study Text Chapter 5 Section 4.2 / CISI Workbook Chapter 7 Section 5

37. **B** The Xetra Dax represents the top 30 German shares

    BPP Study Text Chapter 2 Section 5.2 / CISI Workbook Chapter 4 Section 9

38. **D** For a mortgage with a variable rate, the interest varies in line with the general interest rate climate, and thus would provide a lower interest rate cost if rates fall

    BPP Study Text Chapter 4 Section 6.4 / CISI Workbook Chapter 10 Section 2.4

39. **A** The flat yield is calculated as follows.

    $$\text{Flat yield} = \frac{\text{Gross Coupon}}{\text{Market price}} \times 100$$

    $$= \frac{£6}{£120} \times 100$$

    $$= 5\%$$

    BPP Study Text Chapter 2 Section 9.7 / CISI Workbook Chapter 5 Section 5.3

40. **C** This is an interest in possession trust

    BPP Study Text Chapter 7 Section 8.3 / CISI Workbook Chapter 9 Section 6.3

41. **B** Treasury bills do not pay interest. Instead, they trade at a discount to face value

    BPP Study Text Chapter 2 Section 10.2 / CISI Workbook Chapter 3 Section 3

42. **A** A company can use an interest rate swap to hedge the risk involved in either a fixed or floating rate by accepting the opposite type of rate

    BPP Study Text Chapter 3 Section 5 / CISI Workbook Chapter 6 Section 4.2

43. **D** Net interest is gross interest less tax

    BPP Study Text Chapter 4 Section 1 / CISI Workbook Chapter 3 Section 2

44. **C** Taking the equal but opposite position from the original position is called 'closing out' and effectively extinguishes the obligation to make delivery of the asset at the agreed price and date

    BPP Study Text Chapter 3 Section 2.2 / CISI Workbook Chapter 6 Section 2

45. **A** Equities or shares offer the investor both potential income from dividends and capital growth over time. These are seen as investments for long-term growth

    BPP Study Text Chapter 2 Section 2 / CISI Workbook Chapter 4 Section 4

46. **C** The key word for an option is 'right'

    BPP Study Text Chapter 3 Section 1 / CISI Workbook Chapter 6 Section 3

47. **A** Gilts are exempt from capital gains tax. However, the coupon is subject to income tax at the investor's marginal tax rate

    BPP Study Text Chapter 7 Section 2.2 / CISI Workbook Chapter 9 Section 2.2

48. **B** The fiscal year is the year for which tax assessments are made

    BPP Study Text Chapter 7 Section 1.2 / CISI Workbook Chapter 9 Section 2

49. **B** The Money Laundering Reporting Officer (who may be called the nominated officer) of the firm has this role

    BPP Study Text Chapter 6 Section 2.3 / CISI Workbook Chapter 8 Section 2.1.3

50. **A** The approach is active, unlike index-tracking, which is passive. A high yield approach focuses on stocks that pay relatively high dividends. While value investing may lead the investor to stocks that are unpopular or unfashionable, the approach described is best called 'contrarian'

    BPP Study Text Chapter 5 Sections 1.2 / CISI Workbook Chapter 7 Section 1.3.1